HOW TO INFLUENCE PEOPLE AND DARK PSYCHOLOGY

2-in-1 Book

Proven Manipulation Techniques to Influence Human Psychology. Discover Secret Methods: Body Language, NLP, Deception, Subliminal Persuasion

How to Influence People and Become a Master of Persuasion

Discover Advanced Methods to Analyze People, Control Emotions and Body Language. Leverage Manipulation in Business & Relationship

Table of Contents

Introduction 7
Chapter 1: Manipulation As A Tool Of Masters 9
    The Secrets Of The Greatest Men 10
    The Often Overlooked Human Need To Be Manipulated 12
    Manipulation Is Not Evil, It's Just A Tool 14
Chapter 2: Mastering Your Emotions And Reactions 16
    Know YOURSELF (This Is Key) 16
    Be The Master Of Your Emotions 18
    Develop Your Instincts 21
Chapter 3: Knowledge Of Emotional Reactions And How To Read Them 23
    Knowing Your Mark 24
    Observing And Translating Emotional Reactions 25
    Learn To Take A Clue 26
    To React Or To Obey: The Key To Always Getting It Right 27
    Practice Makes Perfect 28
Chapter 4: Understanding Basic Body Language 29
    Understanding From Less Than Words 30
    The Little Things Are Usually Most Important 34
    Recognizing Tells And Signs Could Be An Art Or Science 35
    Recognizing A Target 35
    Warning Signs 38
Chapter 5: Persuasion: The Psychological Theories (Never Fail To Consider The Target) 40
    The Psychological Perspective 45

Chapter 6: Persuasion: The Practical 48
   Putting The Theories Into Practice 48
   Other Techniques Of Persuasion 52
   Reverse Psychology 56
   Remember To Always Analyze Before Making Your Move 56

Chapter 7: Common Manipulation Techniques 58
   Manipulation Is Not Always For The Faint Hearted 68

Chapter 8: Mastering The Art Of Subtlety-Do Not Be Blatant 70
   The Cautious Approach Is Always Best 70
   A Flimsy Ploy Is Ineffective 71
   Never Get Ahead Of Yourself 72
   Never Go All Out Unless... 72

Chapter 9: Practical Uses of Manipulation 74
   Manipulation in Business 74
   Manipulation In Relationships 76
   Manipulating A Friend 77
   Seductive Manipulation 78
   How To Properly Manipulate Strangers 78

Chapter 10: Manipulating and Scouting: The Forgotten Connection. 80
   Watching Your Target Is Important 80
   Establishing Trust 81
   Planning A Strategy Of Approach 82
   Follow Only What You See Or Hear 83

Conclusion 85

Introduction

There is a belief amongst most people that when sequences and situations are created to change the perception and reactions of a person, it is a negative thing. But if we were to look closely, we would observe that this is something that manifests on a daily basis in our lives. we are constantly trying to change how people see us and the things we do. Sometimes we want them to view us in a positive way and other times in a negative way, depending on what we want to achieve at that moment in time. Some people call this manipulation and it is indeed so but manipulation is not necessarily evil as most people would lead you to believe. Many believe it to be associated with only exploitation and deception for personal gain but fail to praise such tactics when they are used positively in eliminating unhealthy habits and behaviors.

To put this in perspective, do you remember the days when your parents had to promise you gifts and extra play time just to get you to complete your homework? That is manipulation in its simplest form but it doesn't match up with what people like to believe of manipulation. They clearly were not manipulating your reasoning for their own benefit, if anything, it was for yours.

People turn to manipulation for a variety of reasons; to advance their own purposes and agendas, to help you attain your own goals and objectives, to gain power or simply because they find it interesting. The last of these reasons is usually the most dangerous because such people are usually oblivious to the damage they can cause or are already causing until they are too far gone in the game. Such people keep manipulating everyone every time without the slightest hint of guilt. Such people are psychopaths.

This book is has not been produced to turn anyone into a psychopath nor is it written to challenge the status quo of manipulation in the world. It is written to show you the ropes at a skill many already utilize. Yes, everyday people manipulate others; in their business environments, in social settings, in friendships and relationships. So, it is high time you sat down and learnt the tricks to an art that all influential people possess.

Chapter 1: Manipulation As A Tool Of Masters

In the world nowadays, a variety of situations necessitates or determines ascribing someone the title of master. But in all of those situations, the master is the one who has most influence on the people around him or her. The power such a master possesses could have initially been attained by skill or reputation but to avoid losing it over time, the master has to be adept at retaining his or her influence. Such a person is usually held in high regard, regardless of status or wealth and vary rarely do these people attain such a status by being themselves or by being ordinary. Being so might make people to like and admire you but true respect and power over others must be gotten by other means. This is where manipulation comes in.

Manipulation goes hand in hand with power. Wherever you can sense the effect of manipulation, there is bound to be an imbalance of power. The power in such societies is usually concentrated in the hands of a few who could be referred to as masters over others. These people are well versed at making people think along the same lines as them, making people act along the same lines as them, making people follow them unconditionally and generally being able to influence the thoughts and opinions of those around them effectively.

If you were to look back in history at some of the most influential people, one of the things you would observe is that the ideas they advocated were not necessarily moral or even right at all. Their beliefs were not necessarily righteous or ethical, but whenever they needed it, people and followers flocked to their sides, ready to follow them to the end and ready to defend the ideas they had been taught to believe and defend. From terrorist leaders to controversial politicians and men of power who regardless of the revulsion their ideas seemed to generate still seemed to be gaining more power. Why was this so? Because they knew how to influence and control people. It didn't matter what they said but provided they could make people think how they wanted them to and act how they wanted them to, they were never at risk of being powerless. Their power didn't originate from a sense of righteousness or correctness but from the sense of followership they were able to instill in people.

It is this sense of followership and loyalty that you should aim to achieve through manipulation. Manipulation is not just your key to power, it is your key to success because with power comes the ability to thrive off people in any environment. This ability is inherent in all successful people. Whether you are an entrepreneur or someone with a daily job, as long as people are involved, the knowledge of people and how to influence them is necessary for your success.

Some people have those once in a lifetime ideas or a revolutionary approach to solving a problem but without the knowledge of how to thrive on the backs of others, they would never be able to fully consolidate on what they have. The ability to manipulate people is yours to use as you wish; you could use it in your search for personal happiness or in your quest for wealth and affluence, whichever one is your choice. This book, however, has only one aim; helping you become a master in whatever you chose to be or do.

The Secrets Of The Greatest Men

Manipulation and deception are one of the numerous skills possessed by the greatest and most powerful men to have roamed this earth. Not all men are Gandhi and if the history books were properly scoured and its annals scrutinized, many of the men who have exerted the most influence on the world would be shown to be manipulators who merely hid their more negatively perceived talents in a shroud of piety, idealism and oratory.

This is not to say that these men were evil or bad, they just understood the need to do what was necessary when necessary and if this involved tweaking the emotions and thoughts of people to generate reactions that were favorable to their causes, so be it.

And so, the truth behind many of the world's greatest men and leaders is not divine intervention or an alignment of the stars but rather a lack of the emotional restrictions that plague the ordinary man. Many of these men from Caesar to Napoleon weren't evil or psychopathic but had a goal and a vision of the world that couldn't be achieved by simply following the rules and hoping that every other person saw things the same way they did. No, great men do not wait, they act.

Not to limit this to only men, we have had some pretty powerful women in the past who understood that to wield real power was not a matter of honesty or being a good wife but rather how to get people to do what you want when you want it. That is the essence of manipulation, to get people so dependent and so in awe of you that you could easily influence their principles and guide their actions in the direction you believe it ought to be going in. Take for instance, the sexual manipulation of both Caesar and Mark Anthony by Cleopatra in a bid to protect her interests and titles. It is mostly overlooked but that has in no way detracted from her brilliant manipulation of two very powerful men.

What I am trying to say here is that many of the events that have shaped the world politically, industrially, even religiously are so mired in manipulation, it's hard to dismiss its usefulness in both the old days and the modern world. It is used as a business tactic, as a means of motivation or as an aid to persuasion in almost any facet of life.

In the modern world, manipulation is synonymous with politics and is widely thought to be used only by politicians, business executives and the likes but if you look closely, you would see that we all practice a form of manipulation. In fact, any setting in which there seems to be an imbalance of power probably contains an element of manipulation and since this imbalance in power is a staple of the realistic world, it could be said that manipulation is rife in the world and in our everyday life. There is manipulation in our daily interactions, in our personal relationships, our business relationships and even religious interactions. Consider the clergy who spends a large chunk of his sermon emphasizing on punishment of sin and the travails of hell, he might be speaking the truth but his words are meant to impart fear in you and it is that fear which he counts on to make the difference in your approach to life. That is a classic case of emotional manipulation using fear. The cleric does not mean to do this but deep down he realizes that this is the most effective way of knocking into people the need for his or her God. He does not mean to manipulate you but he does it nonetheless. That is what manipulation is. You might truly respect the autonomy of a person but when you feel you need to influence them, you could unknowingly find yourself trying to take advantage of their emotions and this means you are manipulating them. You do not have to be evil, you simply need to recognize the necessity for a line of action and possess the strength of mind to do what needs to be done.

Over the course of this book, you would learn how to wield similar power over people, how to make yourself indispensable and how to make yourself capable of greatness.

The Often Overlooked Human Need To Be Manipulated

As humans we have all been blessed with autonomy, the right to make our own decisions and live by them and any threat to such autonomy generally has us on guard. That is the reason why when faced with anything, law or person we believe aims to rip this independence from us, we fight back with or without violence. Take into consideration the numerous uprisings in history as proof of this. The people who led the French and English revolutions did not possess more power than the monarchs in power but when they felt their needs being thrown out the door and their independence being preyed upon, they fought back and they fought hard.

Our history when it comes to defending our independence is quite rich, from the early advocates of our modern religions facing up to the idol worshippers in their day to the women throughout history who have fought for equal rights. They might not have realized what they were doing but they were exercising an innate human need to be free. But just as the need to be free exists, so does the need to be controlled or the need for order.

This need to be controlled is the reason why humans needed monarchs and governments to rule and govern their daily life. Because if left to live life freely and unchecked, we would have been consumed by chaos. But as our population grew and we expanded to cover more territory, so did the influence of such monarchs and governments, the controlling forces, on our life wear thin, eventually becoming insignificant. Though this is on a much grander scale and might, it is a larger manifestation of our need to sometimes be guided by others. Thus, it is apt to say that every one of us needs guidance.

The guidance might be spiritual, academic or psychological but if we were to trace the source of our knowledge, we would find that it must have originated from a person or book and very rarely is it completely original. To better understand this, consider how you always feel the need to try and impart the knowledge you have unto others either by holding lectures or by giving advice. This need to guide one another is how we humans have passed our knowledge over millenniums.

It is because of this inherent need for guidance, knowledge and control that we are susceptible to manipulation. I am not saying that anybody deserves to be manipulated but that everybody can be manipulated. And since whatever is possible is always done, the possibility of being manipulated means that some of us, or rather, many of us are bound to fall victim to people whose goal is to manipulate us. It is the way of the world, the only difference between you and the next person is how good you are at it and how you want to use your influence and skill.

Manipulation Is Not Evil, It's Just A Tool

It is widely believed that manipulation is evil, I neither support nor assent to this belief. Manipulation is the use of any sort of influence, be it physical, emotional or financial, over a person, group or situation to generate a desired outcome. The outcome is most likely one which favors you and your goals but does not necessarily need to be detrimental to other people involved. On another note, the belief of manipulation being negative usually assumes that this goal you want to achieve is not in sync with that of your mark or target. But, what if it does? Won't it then be more apt to classify your manipulation as a means of motivation or, at the very least, as a positive influence? Consider this:

You have a boss who is hell bent on following a particular line of action as regards a new business deal yet facts and your gut tell you that his approach or decision is a wrong one. But he refuses to listen to the opinions of anyone, probably because his stance is as a result of a very old sentiment or bias. In this case, every straightforward and honest approach has failed. Wouldn't it be better to manipulate and tweak his emotions just a little bit and save his job and the company's balance sheet from recording a loss?

In such a case, your manipulation of your boss is still considered immoral but on the general balance of events, it is the right course of action if all means of rational persuasion have been exhausted. From a conventional point of view, the idea of one person manipulating another is considered a criticism of the manipulator's behavior, but is manipulation always immoral? The above example doesn't seem immoral. When looked at on a grander scale, we would most likely agree that manipulation is rife in our everyday life but the only times it is actually classified as evil or bad is when it leads to harm, be it emotional or psychological, of the target. Sure, manipulation can expose vulnerabilities that otherwise might have remained hidden. Yes, manipulation could lead to oppression of people but it could also be the only way to achieve a truly noble goal. Consider this next example.

Assuming you are a security officer who was unlucky enough to be on duty on the day a terrorist was captured and you have credible intel that the terrorist is slated to carry out an attack on that very day or maybe during the week. You have tried every possible method of rational reasoning from trying to tap into his or her empathy to offering deals but the terrorist has refused to budge and the only way to extract the information without resorting to violence is to employ manipulation as a tool. Is this considered immoral or is the immorality simply justified simply because you get to save many lives?

Depending on your answer to the above question, the knowledge shared in this book might one day be beneficial to you. If you possess a hardline view on the perception of manipulation and are of the opinion that it can never be used for a positive goal, the knowledge of this book is of no practical use to you and you are better served stopping here and picking a book that is more acceptable and is less likely to offend your sensibilities.

Chapter 2: Mastering Your Emotions And Reactions

Manipulation is a game of emotions, knowing how to read them, how to tweak them, how to play them, erase them, create them and react to them. Every manipulative move should be aimed at exposing the emotional core of your mark or target because that is the only way to owning their actions and decisions. But for you to adequately and efficiently effect your desired change in the individual or group of relevance, you have to have an understanding of yourself and your emotions. To put it cleanly, you have to know yourself more than any other person because only then can you make a move at controlling others.

Know YOURSELF (This Is Key)

Knowing yourself is key if not the most important ingredient to possess before you embark on the road to mastering people. This is because, to avoid overreaching or underestimating yourself, you have to possess an understanding of your abilities, a keen sense as to where your strengths end and where your weaknesses begin. Only with this knowledge can you decipher the direction in which you should be leading your mark and the approach you should be taking to do so.

Such in depth knowledge of oneself would require a level of truthfulness in accepting one's limitations and a further level of self-discipline to avoid crossing those limits. The idea behind getting under your target's defenses would vary depending on the target but would require you to either play up your weaknesses while emphasizing your strengths or play up your strengths while emphasizing your weaknesses. Both require you to be alert.

How To Influence People

As important as understanding your limits is, it would be nothing without an understanding of your emotions and that would be incomplete without the ability to recognize your emotional markers. These markers are what people see regardless of what goes on in your head and thus, are more likely to influence their thoughts. This knowledge is not achieved by simply making a resolution but by logically analyzing your every move in a bid to pinpoint how your internal emotions manifest as external actions. This might seem complex but it is actually quite easy. It just involves thinking about your reactions and emotion as two separate entities then following them through step by step to the end and figuring out how one influences the other. Let me give you a hypothetical situation.

A friend of yours who is usually quiet and reserved walks up to you one day and shoves you in the back in a moment of excitement. It was a playful shove but you not realizing it were this particular friend turns back and are about to express your anger before you notice him and check yourself. He sees this and wonders why you would react in such a way and in a playful manner shoves you again. This time however, you don't check yourself but instead launch into a tirade.

At the time he hit you the first time, let's assume you were in a rather normal state, not particularly angry or happy. After the first hit, you got angry but controlled yourself. While this control is necessary to possess for the skill you are learning, the important part of your analysis should be what gave your anger away since you had not actually reacted. You have to know if it was a clenched fist by your side, a hardened facial expression, a twitching eye or whatever because controlling the reaction is only half the lesson, you have to behave outwardly like the thought of a reaction never even crossed your mind. This is the kind of logical breakdown you must grow adept at performing on yourself and your actions. You must abandon the ordinary man's habits of reacting impulsively and start reacting logically. Next, you have to consider your loss of control on the succeeding incident. Such a reaction could point to the shove itself being an act that ticks you off, an underlying problem or problems with the aforementioned friend or even your limit in such situations. Whichever one it is, you need to get a handle on it and eliminate all emotions from your reactions unless when you feel it has to be released.

Be The Master Of Your Emotions

Other than your strengths and weaknesses, another key area of your life and being to pay attention to is your emotions. Most people underestimate the need for a control over their emotions and that is the major reason they have little control over the emotions of others. I am not advising for you to remain meek regardless of the provocation or for you to flare up at the slightest sign of resistance. No, what I am saying is that you have to be able to control whatever reaction is necessary in the moment, to bring it out at a moment's notice and to lock it back up when it has served its purpose. You need to recognize your emotional triggers and work at dulling their effect. Failing at such an important facet of your person could lead you to unwillingly push a target too far or to allow a target run wild and free for too long. Meanwhile, mastering the control of your emotion in this way would give the double advantage of reducing the ability people possess to rile you up or manipulate you while also granting you complete autonomy over your own reactions.

As I implied earlier, different targets require different approaches and different treatments and for this reason different emotions would elicit different effects on them. Where anger might cause one to be subservient, it might cause another to be more belligerent. This is the major reason you have to master not just the ability to act and create emotional reactions but also the ability to suppress your more natural emotional reactions as these said reactions can interfere with the image you are trying to portray.

Your control on your emotions is one of the major tools by which you control the perception people have of you and when it comes to manipulating people, it is key that you control their perception of you because only then would you control how they will treat you. It is important for you to remember that the initial way by which people judge another's character is through his or her behavior and emotional disposition and as such, control over both would grant onto you the power to control people's perception of you.

From another angle, your emotional disposition towards issues and events is usually a cornerstone of your reputation, at least in the minds of most people. This is a weakness in people. They assume that emotions are almost unchangeable thereby nullifying the possibility in their minds that one is capable of manipulating his or her emotions to deceive them. They believe that your reaction to a situation would always stay constant unless another effect is in play. The trick is introducing another reaction/emotion that contradicts your normal in a bid to gain their attention while lowering their defenses to deal with your perceived soft spot.

Because of this nullification, this is a belief you must always be out to take advantage of. The warning behind this is that before attempting to cash in on this mistake, you have to have fine-tuned your ability to act out scenarios and create emotions. If you are not well versed at this, a smart target might figure out your play before you are even started.

Furthermore, when utilizing this weakness, the emotion being introduced should be as evanescent as possible so as not to confuse the target. What I mean is that, with such a tactic, the effect you are going for is the **"oh, that is so unlike him"** effect and not the **"oh, he has changed so much from the time we met"** effect. This means that the emotion to be introduced should be temporary and fleeting, only surfacing for a brief period of time. Most times, the tactic is effective for a particular emotion only once or twice and should never be attempted consecutively using the same emotion. Here is an illustration of this particular trick.

The target is a female and you have gone through the basics with her, establishing a character and manufacturing reactions for every predictable action of hers. In your bid to seduce her, you have gotten to first base, first kiss and now you are looking to score a big finish and leave. But she's been very coy and defensive about sex and you haven't been able to lower her defenses on the issue. One day an issue comes up between you guys and ordinarily you would have let it slide with a smile but instead you flare up for a bit and take to keeping to yourself. She avoids bringing up the issue for a while but later comes in for the conversation.

The major point here is the change from your regular emotional reaction to a more aggressive one. This would prompt her to believe that you might have lost a little bit of emotional control and seeing as such instability is a constant source of discussion in relationships, your current countenance would require her to have a conversation with you. Bear in mind that the conversation is not for you to petulantly complain about her not having sex with you but rather for you to make her feel she is in a position of power to broker peace while considering you to be the victim. You are not to make things overly hard or easy for her. Your time to act would come after you have settled the quarrel. It would be right for you to initiate a make out session rather than ask her to have sex. This moment in which she has lowered her defenses to accommodate your emotional issues is when you make your move and if you have played your cards right up to that moment, you are about to get that score you have been hoping for. From then onwards, it is up to you to proceed as you wish but with smarts of course. Do not forget, overusing this tactic increases the possibility of exposing your game to your target.

Develop Your Instincts

Instincts are natural; they are either borne from experience or you are born with them. It is that voice in your head that speaks to you when you are in a fix and need a quick solution to your problem. It is the one that guides most of your impulsive reactions. I bet you used to doubt your impulses could change but trust me they can. Many people believe impulses can only be controlled but that is for someone who still wants to possess impulses. Real masters of emotions do not just control their impulses, they eliminate them. Only when those impulses are absent do the instincts you have trained yourself in start to kick in.

Our instincts are a product of our deeper nature, our deeper understanding and our environment. They usually mirror the things we have learnt and experienced. When we act on our instincts, were basically surrendering to our past experiences and innermost directions. These directions can be changed but not easily. To truly develop your instincts is not a matter of turning pages or staring at a screen and absorbing words but rather putting your skills to the test in real life and facing failure because only with these can you correct the folly of past experiences and create new directions. You have to put your newly learned tactics to work, feel them out, recognize how to make them click for you and depending on what you succeed or fail at, your mind will automatically store all of these experiences as either positive results inducing actions or negative results inducing actions. It is based on the presence of this more advanced knowledge that your instincts become sharper and more trustworthy because you stop making decisions steeped in theoretical propaganda and start making experienced decisions.

Instincts are necessary in understanding people and situations because only when you know what to look out for can you correctly react but in instances when the mark is still more of a stranger, you have to rely on your instincts and experiences to guess what type of person you are dealing with in terms of temperament, likes, dislikes, potential tells and the likes. Without the necessary sharp instincts, these would be quite difficult if not impossible.

Chapter 3: Knowledge Of Emotional Reactions And How To Read Them

Reading people is arguably the most vital tool to a successful manipulation. This might be an art to some or a science to others depending on if they are naturally talented at it or if it is a completely acquired skill. Don't get me wrong, I do not mean to say that some are born with the ability to read people. What I mean is that it comes easier to some people with time than others.

Reading people and their emotions is a historically difficult task and yet without it, attempting a manipulation is akin to a blind man climbing a mountain. Many believe it to be about making snap decisions based on how people look and jumping to conclusions before you have even shared a word but in truth, it is way more than that. Before we jump into this, I should warn you that psychologists have confirmed that there is no foolproof way to read or decipher people and I would like to personally add that many of the methods you might learn might seem contradictory. Having said this, it is up to you to engage your wits and let your instincts guide you.

A key facet of reading people is their emotional disposition towards various situations. To really understand them through this means, you need to have watched them react to a few situations so as to give you a feel as to how they might react in similar and contrasting settings. However, emotions are notoriously difficult to decipher and many amateurs make the mistake of translating signs and gestures into singular meanings. This is wrong because a sign could denote multiple possible emotions.

It is due to this possibility that signs and gestures should not be treated or read as individual entities but rather should be taken contextually, while also putting into consideration other facts available to you. The last ingredient that is needed to make the result of a reading as close to reality as possible is a sharp instinct. I have spoken about developing this in chapter 2 and will refrain from discussing further but in my opinion, it is the most important tool for reading people.

Knowing Your Mark

The first step to reading a mark or target is to abandon all of your previous projections and prejudices about people. These prejudices could be racial, ethnic etc. but they should all be thrown out because without a clean slate on which to present your facts, you risk destroying your readings with bias and sentiments. As a manipulator, your main goal in reading people, especially strangers, is not to spot deceit but to spot openings which could be used to forge connections or to discover character traits that could be used to your advantage. I would advise that when initially attempting manipulations, you pick targets that are more insecure, lonely or are possessing of low self-esteem. This is usually obvious from their need to defend themselves regularly, an eagerness to join or participate in a conversation, shyness, tendency to back down from confrontations and similar behaviors.

A general way to get people to initially lower their defenses with you is to act charming. Do not act all weird and slimy with them but adopt a natural witty charm, the kind reserved for your principal or favorite high school teacher back in the day. This is especially effective with shy or insecure targets, people who would welcome compliments and are more likely to warm to jokes and strangers faster.

Another way is to break down the trust barrier by offering a little of yourself and your secrets first. This part of you doesn't necessarily have to be true but it must be believable. Once the primary connection is formed however, it is time to begin information gathering. If your mark is talkative, you are in luck. Simply keep quiet and let the prattle run. There is bound to be at least a tidbit of information scattered in between. However, if the target is more reserved or quieter, a little bit of skillful prodding is needed to tap into the right vibe and once you get it, be sure to keep the buzz going for as long as possible.

Other than information garnered from conversation, you can also proceed to watch the crowd he/she hangs out with, her favorite drinks, favorite color and hobbies. This might seem very banal but knowledge of them could give you an in with the mark and that's all that is needed to improve your status in their lives. Once you have established the right relationship, the next step is to hunt for the more private bits of information, the ones most likely to push the buttons you need pushed.

Observing And Translating Emotional Reactions

To properly observe a person's reactions and understand the logic or motive behind them, you have to take an objective perspective of the person's actions, devoid of any connections whatsoever. To do this you first have to establish the nature of the events or situations causing such a reaction to check for its conventionality because since most people tend to react conventionally to certain things, the abnormalities and oddities are the ones to look out for. Next, you analyze the markers of these reactions in the person so that if such a reaction were to occur for another stimulus, it would be clear what such a person is feeling. Some emotions may possess the same marker and would therefore require secondary markers or experience with the target to tell them apart.

The need for marking the emotional reaction of the target as well as its causes is to be well placed to use the emotions to your advantage. Also knowing the tells would expose to you the presence of a particular emotion, allowing you to adapt to the mood and needs of the person thus keeping yourself relevant while making them believe that you care. This might probably only be necessary at the beginning of the association as the person is more likely to show more subservience or dependence as the manipulations grows deeper.

Deciphering and translating the emotions of a person might seem tricky at first but usually gets easier with time. For instance, staying with a new cousin, family relative or roommate might be difficult at first but as you start to warm up to them and learn about their eccentricities, what makes them tick and what kills their buzz, their secrets begin to up to you one at a time. It's the same way with targets of manipulations; you need to invest time in understanding and learning their reactions and what they mean so as to avoid pushing the wrong buttons at the wrong times.

Learn To Take A Clue

Very rarely, you might encounter an oddity that more or less does not conform to the reading you have arrived at on a particular person, do not fret and do not react too swiftly. It is better to ignore it outwardly while watching for signs of repetition. The smart play would be to analyze it, try to understand what brought about the anomaly and if it is likely to happen again. This is necessary because manipulation is about control of not only the target but of everything affecting the target that can be controlled. Those that cannot be controlled should be predicted and skillfully avoided to prevent any surprises from occurring.

Take for example, you have cultivated a manipulative relationship with a young lady or man who is quite reserved and is more prone to long periods of silence. Then on a night out together, the target completely flips script and goes all wild partygoer on you, do not react hastily. It could be as a result of something or someone in their life that you are not familiar with and a hasty reaction against a previously entrenched stimulus could be rather counterproductive. Instead, it would be advisable for you go along with the flow and later question their behavior. This would enable you to gain the knowledge you want without relinquishing control of the situation.

This is the idea behind taking a clue. You have to be ready to adapt and shift your position to better understand a situation.

To React Or To Obey: The Key To Always Getting It Right

This is one of my favorite rules because it requires patient thinking and smart decision making. The translation is rather simple. To react is to adopt an active approach while to obey is to do otherwise. The rule applies to you, the manipulator, and the target. It is simply used to stop impulsive action. The question is quite straightforward, do you react to a situation or let things slide?

This question is one you should never fail to ask yourself before putting another ploy in motion. It would be reckless of you if you were to move too fast and sloppy of you if you were to move too slowly. That is where the question comes in. It challenges you to consider your status and decide if any further action is necessary. Failure to make the right choice often ends in regret.

An alternative question, mostly used at the beginning of a manipulation to better gauge the chances of success of the ploy, is to ask yourself how smart your target truly is. This might seem ordinary but for you to succeed you have to have complete faith in your own abilities while steering clear of overconfidence and most times a good perception of the targets own intellect is the perfect constraint.

As effective as this rule could be, there is no trick or shortcut to knowing the answer to the question. To react or to obey could only be answered by you. You are to put every piece of information you possess on the target into play and then consult your gut and instincts on whether one or the other is the right choice. You would probably stumble a few times during the learning process but you could also be a natural, getting it right every single time. Whichever it is, remember to always learn from your experiences because only through our experiences are we ever truly equipped to deal with the future.

Practice Makes Perfect

As previously stated, manipulation has to be worked at constantly to attain the level at which success becomes the norm. Practice and constant use of the skills you learn would sharpen your skills as regards people and how they should be dealt with. All the advice in this book are merely words on a piece of paper or an audio recording without your own ability to bring them to life. Everyone is different and as such, different methods work for them. This applies to you as much as it applies to your target. You have to be able to bring the ideas in this book in a way that suits your character and approach and there is no better way to learn to do this than by practicing.

Manipulation is a game that deals with emotions and constant practice is perfect to boost your instincts as well as your confidence. Stick to these rules and warning and it's only a matter of time before you become a master manipulator. Just like in every other field, without sharp instincts, you are ordinary, without experience you carry a large chance of failure, without confidence you can do nothing. Practice is important if you are to achieve all three and rise above being ordinary.

Chapter 4: Understanding Basic Body Language

When two people meet each other, it doesn't matter whether they are old friends or new acquaintances, they could even be strangers, but they communicate through not only words but gestures. These gestures tend to betray our mental state and express how we are feeling. For instance, if were feeling bad and irritable, we give off defensive signals and when we are feeling happy, we tend to be more relaxed and friendlier.

These gestures and signals relay our mood to the person or persons around us and affects what they think and how they relate with us at that moment in time. This ability to read basic and common gestures is rather inherent in every one but as a result of practice and experience some people are more adept at it than others. For example, women are generally more perceptive to gestures than men, probably due to the fact that they might have had lots of practice dealing with their kids or those of others.

Many common gestures such as crying, laughing and frowning denote the same emotional and mental state in most people with very little exceptions. However, your emphasis on body language and gestures as a manipulator should go beyond the study of the more common gestures if you hope to become a master. It should at least encompass the knowledge of basic body language for you to truly appreciate its effect on your everyday choices and decisions. You should also be able to notice and translate a wide range of uncommon expressions.

Gestures and signals could mean many things in different places, so it would be wise to observe the general trends around wherever you stay and ask questions when necessary before jumping to needless conclusions. Furthermore, the frequencies with which these gestures occur vary with a variety of factors. One of these is age. It has been proven that the older people get the lesser the gestures they use in communicating their opinions. Another factor is wealth or social class. It has also been noticed that people higher up the social chain in a particular environment use fewer gestures than those below them. These are all generalizations and exceptions to such are bound to occur. For example, people who are very excited tend to gesticulate more and those who are bored, take on a more reserved demeanor. Thus, a bored teenager could probably use less gestures and body movement in expressing him or herself than an excited septuagenarian. In such a case, the age generalization would have failed.

Well, other than these generalizations, it is important to pay attention to the particular gestures of each person while also monitoring their verbal output. Look for contradictions that give the person away as regards whether they are lying or hiding something and make your next steps based on these deductions. The most effective way of catching lying in a person is to watch out for gestures that betray their true intention. Such gestures or behaviors are usually out of place or out of sync with the message they are delivering or trying to deliver.

Understanding From Less Than Words

The ability to tell as much as possible about a person without engaging in conversations is one that would help you well, especially when it comes to securing and developing a new target. When I say developing a target, I mean the first few conversations and meetings you have in which you try to determine the attitude and emotional disposition of the person towards key issues so as to better mold the character you would assume around them.

This understanding of a person could aid your quest in many ways. It could portray you as someone who is perceptive and sensitive to their need and this is a good way of establishing trust within the target. It could also be useful in predicting the actions of a person so as to better react to them. This reaction could be in many forms varying from a modified approach to a subject to a complete avoidance of another. It is, in summary, a good way to avoid falling afoul of a person before you have been able to achieve what you initially set out to achieve.

Many signs could actually mean more than one thing and should not be taken as a complete truth but rather as a possible truth. What this means is that, all possible translations should be considered before you jump to any final conclusions. This is due to the fact that more than one factor could be in play and probably the telling factor causing a particular reaction is not even from us but from another person or situation entirely. Such consideration should apply to both positive and negative reactions because we, as humans, tend to apply this to only the negatives while imagining all positive reactions to be of our own making. I am going to consider the reactions we should or could expect in a first meeting because I assume that after the first meeting, your status or likely status should be established already. Let us begin with reactions to expect in a first meeting.

1. Acceptance and rejection: Being able to perceive whether someone is digging you or accepting your approach is quite important as it tells you a lot about the success of your current approach on the person and whether or not you may need to change it. Though it is very difficult to know if your message is getting through, little gestures such as moving closer and interrupting every now and then to put in a point should bolster your confidence that your presence is at least not unwanted. In fact, if you really want to judge whether or not your company is pleasing to the person, it would be more apt to look for the signals of rejection rather than those of acceptance. You should look for signs such as how regularly the person offers an opinion during a conversation, how frequently and how sincerely the person smiles or laughs at your jokes, whether the person retreats whenever you move closer and how long the person spends in a side conversation with another friend before returning to you and whether or not they apologize.

The regularity with which the person offers opinions show how much the person is concentrating on your words and this in turn denotes if and how interesting your company is. If the person speaks only a little, it could mean that the person doesn't like you or is bored. Anyhow, if walking away is not an option, you could resort to asking a question and using the persons answer to change the topic. Watch out for changes in their reactions to gauge their concentration.

Someone who laughs frequently and sincerely at your jokes is definitely enjoying the conversation and is less likely to leave soon. However, someone who just stares at you after a joke or gives a weak smile is probably not impressed by you or your wit. But before jumping to conclusions, the blank stare could also be as a result of a lack of understanding on their part.

If after a few moments of a conversation, you attempt to lean in to emphasize a point and the target (mostly females in this case) retreats, taking a step or two back, it could mean that she doesn't like you, she still considers you a stranger, she is surprised or she simply isn't feeling the conversation as much as you thought. it might even be due to mouth odor. The trick with dealing with this is to stay calm and pretend not to notice this. Continue with the conversation as naturally as possible and after a few minutes, attempt to lean in again. If she retreats again, it is probably due to one of the first two possible reasons or the mouth odor.

During conversations with a person, it is quite common for side conversations with a passing friend to occur. The duration of this side conversation could however be of significance when it comes to determining how they view you. If the side conversation goes on for so long that you look and feel like you are standing all alone and yet the person with whom you were conversing hasn't offered an apology, the meaning is quite bad. But if the person constantly cuts short the side conversation to apologize to you an even takes the hard decision of cutting short and postponing such a conversation, it means your presence is at least appreciated and not unwanted. If the former was actually the case, it could be due to the fact that the target considers your presence to be boring, and the side conversation to be a needed reprieve. If this is so walk away and do not return, unless the target approaches you. Save your dignity.

2. Happiness: Someone who immediately warms up to you in a first meeting or conversation and is happy to have your company would most likely participate in the conversation, not just butting in to express opinions but also to tell stories and crack jokes. Such a person is also likely to laugh a lot and may even attempt to introduce you to a few more people if you are a stranger at whatever place you are meeting. It is also possible that the person is intoxicated and their overly positive reaction is due to whatever intoxicant they might have ingested. The best way to deal with this is to go on with the flow and probably try getting their contact information for a future meeting but keeping whatever conclusions you may have had aside for when such a meeting comes. A distant possibility is that they are utilizing your company to achieve a goal of their own, say, making someone jealous. I classified this as a distant possibility because it rarely happens but I still felt the need to mention it so as to stress the need for you to always consider all options and to always stay aware of everything going on around you and your target.

3. Distaste or dislike: This is different from rejection in that the person in this case would probably not even be polite enough to answer you properly. It is rather easy to spot and could include signs like a frown, lack of eye contact and short or monosyllabic answers. If this happens to you, do not inquire as to what might be wrong or what you might have done wrong. Instead, say your goodbyes and walk away. If you are to approach such a person again, be sure to have a friend of theirs there to introduce you first. This could make all the difference.

The possible scenarios are endless but these are the most popular reactions you could come up against. The reason for outlining these situations and how to deal with them is to enable you use the knowledge of basic body language and how to properly react to them to better make a first conversation or meeting as fruitful as possible. If dealing with failure and rejection is not a strong point of yours, it might be better to watch from a distance how such a person relates with others and judge using these same skills, how to approach such a person or if he or she is worth the stress.

The Little Things Are Usually Most Important

We have touched on some of the more elaborate and obvious gestures and the little ones are up next. These are called little because they are mostly imperceptible and are done very quickly. They are those things one is likely to miss or overlook such as a quick lick of the lip, a glance at a wristwatch or clock, a glance at another person or even running a hand through their hair. These things are likely to possess meanings that are particular to different people and as such, the same meaning might not apply to different people. These types of reactions should not be studied and translated as individual events or reaction but instead as a part of a larger one.

To adequately guess the meaning to this sort of reactions, you need to consider other gestures that might have come immediately before it, what the target was saying at the moment of the reaction and any possible contradictions between the two. The truth is such reactions rarely occur only once. Most times they are conditioned reflexes in the person to help them deal with something they are otherwise uncomfortable with. It is equally as rare for anyone to recognize any of these reactions not to talk of translating it without spending a tremendous amount of time with the person. For this reason, such reactions are psychological gold and should be cherished.

These inherent reactions are what we call tells.

Recognizing Tells And Signs Could Be An Art Or Science

The ability to instantly recognize a tell or sign in a person when you see one could be an in born or a developed attribute. one could simply spend a few weeks with people and be able to reveal three or four tells that point to how the target is really feeling while other spend years and still struggle to recognize one. This is no reason to worry because while the ability to notice and translate tells makes manipulation easier, the absence of such a skill doesn't make it impossible. Having said this, it should be noted that recognizing such tells can be learnt so, if you lack the natural knack for seeing them, you can still manipulate your target but knowing how to recognize some would definitely be advantageous.

Some tells could be the tendency for a person to run his or her hands through the hair, crossing of the fingers, rapid blinking, twitching of the eye, rapping the knuckles on a surface and many others. These seem like actions that denote rather obvious emotions but most tells are. The major issue with a tell is that these obvious actions do not actually follow an easily perceivable emotion and are usually done so quickly, they could be mistaken for necessary. Thus, to notice them, one must be observant and to translate them, you might have a good grasp of whatever situation them might have occurred under. Isolating the situation and breaking it down into a list of potential stimuli could help in narrowing down the possible meanings.

Recognizing A Target

One of the most important things for being a good manipulator is the ability to notice the right people, the ability to pick the right targets. Well, sorry, there are no right targets. The truth is that everyone can be manipulated by a master but it takes a lot of practice to become a master and as such, for beginners like you, picking the easy or more susceptible targets is the smarter move.

Generally speaking, the easiest people to manipulate are usually those with low self-esteem, low self-confidence or other form of insecurities. These traits usually manifest in numerous forms and it is these forms you have to be trained to notice.

- **Naivety:** This is a very popular draw for manipulation because the victim is almost never aware that he or she possesses such a trait and this limits the possibility that they will eventually discover you. It could be noticed clearly in people who always strive to see the best in others. Such a person even when confronted with the idea and even evidence of manipulation is likely to still believe everything is a coincidence and should have another explanation. This is definitely one you should look out for.

- **Emotional dependence:** People who exhibit this trait are almost always in relationships and such relationships are almost always ending. Why is this? Because their happiness depends on the happiness of others and due to this, they could be considered needy. But their neediness is to your advantage. These sorts of people would do anything to keep you happy, even if it goes against their best interests and the best thing is, they'd do it quite willingly. This would mean little effort from you and an almost servile target. The only caveat to this type of person is that, they are mostly always the jealous types. Be careful.

- **Low self-confidence:** If you have ever met someone with low self-confidence, you'd agree with me that they are always seeking validation of their actions and decisions and these tend to expose them to manipulation. As a manipulator, your power over this class of people lies in your approval and the way you use it. Withholding such an approval makes them eager, to please and giving the approval makes them happy, relaxed and ripe for the taking.

- **Pseudo-manipulators:** Have you ever met people who like to feel like they are the smartest and the most powerful in the room? If yes, this is their class. People like this usually feel like they can prey on others and are good manipulators but in truth are nothing but failures. They are very hard to find but if you ever meet a person who acts out manipulative tendencies but possesses no real influence on people, you have your mark. The way to handle such people is to play the victim or subordinate and strive to avoid doing their wishes while making sure they do yours. This might involve a whole lot of acting and a few concessions at the beginning but would definitely be worth the hassle at the end. These people are mostly narcissists and are easy to pick out using this very trait.
- **Lack of assertiveness:** These kinds of people do not have the ability to make up their mind and this is a weakness to take advantage off. You should strive to play the role of bully or higher authority, someone who makes decisions for them. Provided you play up your best decisions while hiding your worst, you are bound to stay in their lives and stay in control.
- **Altruism:** This is one of those traits that are present in people who show a high level of honesty, fairness and empathy, emphasis on the empathy. This is the emotion to go after as it blinds the target to your true nature and makes him more likely to buy into your act. This makes he/ she susceptible to your talents but not foolish, so you'd still have to play your cards right to have the desired impact.

There are many other traits to look out for and with time and experience, you'd discover them. Looking closely, you would notice that at least one of these traits is present in everyone you know. This is the reason why everyone, even yourself can be manipulated and as such, while playing your game, never drop your guard and always be on the lookout in case your target is also playing a game on you. I should also add that while these traits make people more susceptible to manipulation, your abilities and skills are the factors that would truly determine if the manipulation would be successful or not.

Warning Signs

Everybody can be manipulated but some people are less likely to fall than others. If you are a beginner and you are just learning the ropes, it is necessary for you to avoid individuals high up on the 'less likely' list. To achieve this, you need to know the particular traits or character types to look out for. Such people are:

- **The stubborn:** They are not impossible to break but are better avoided because they might cost too much effort. Stubborn people are usually hard to manipulate because they have self-created opinions, whose tenets they uphold strictly. Worse is the fact that they are prone to arguing a lot and seeing as this is rather inherent in them, it is a trait you would have to figure a way around if you plan on sticking around. Except you are very confident you can get the job done, steer clear.
- **Insensitive people:** This type lacks the ability to feel much in terms of empathy or sympathy and only care about their own interests. You might think that's a good thing but remember, their wellbeing is most likely top of their worries and any sign of manipulation is sure to set off alarm bells.
- **Immature people:** Immaturity is normally a trait that should set people out for manipulation because it is a close sibling of naivety. However, most immature people possess the ability to hold grudges for a tremendous period of time and you do not want them hunting you down for hurting their feelings or

stealing their properties. They tend to make very determined enemies. The stubborn also possess this tendency.

- **People with close friends and relatives:** The best targets are usually those who reside far away from most family and friends because this reduces the chances of trusted outside forces trying to undo your work. Unless, you can think of a way to wean your target off such influence or at least factor them into your plans, the ploy is going to be extremely difficult to pull off. Even if you are ready to manipulate the entire group, ask yourself if it is worth the effort.

Chapter 5: Persuasion: The Psychological Theories (Never Fail To Consider The Target)

Persuasion is a deliberate effort to change or alter a person's opinions, beliefs or attitude toward a particular issue, situation, object or person. This is usually achieved by transmission of a message which could be verbal or symbolic.

While persuasion could be used in a manipulative sense, it is in actual sense different from manipulation. This is because, when persuading a person, he/she is usually aware of your efforts at changing their point of view and willingly or reluctantly allows you to try. In this instance, the person listens and concentrates on what you are saying and then tries to rationalize your ideas with reality before then putting whatever conclusions they come to comparison with what they previously believed.

Your role in the entire dynamic is to state your reasons for the change you are prescribing, give illustrations and evidence supporting your views and try to convince the target of your advances that your line of action or advice is their best bet. The main goal of this is getting them to switch to a state of reasoning or a product that you prefer. It is in this that persuasion resembles manipulation. Because your goal is still to push the target towards an outcome that they might ordinarily not have considered right.

The success attained in persuasion usually depends on the preconceptions held by the target and their strength, their perception of the person sharing the new message or idea, their perception of the message or idea and finally, their perception of the conclusion on offer. Upon outlining these reasons, it should be clear to you that the subject of your effort would probably possess ideas that are at least dissimilar, if not contradictory, to yours and as such the entire process would either hinge on your persuasion being very convincing or the ability of the target to meet a compromise between the conflicting ideas that would majorly mirror the changes you want.

Below are six major theories that strive to explain the way the human mind absorbs and reacts to information. Knowledge of these would greatly increase the odds of persuasion if you could pinpoint it in your target.

- **The attribution theory:** This concludes that people would either attribute actions and characters to people or object respectively either in relation to the context they are being considered in or according to their own emotional disposition.

  When they attribute using context as a guide, they are likely to come to decisions that take into consideration environment of origin and situational factors. Such is seen when a person refrains from calling a product inferior or calling a person insensitive, instead arguing that the product has been made from the best possible items available to the manufacturer and that the person is simply reacting as he has learnt to from his childhood environment.

  However, when considering their own emotional disposition, they tend to believe that whatever is convenient for them is the only right decision or approach for every other person. Consider this situation:
  You meet a person at an event or gathering and try starting a conversation with them but instead of giving you a polite audience, the person appears preoccupied with their own thoughts or acts aloof. Angered or annoyed, you walk away and when asked for an opinion on the person, you characterize them as proud, arrogant or self-important.

In this case, the characterization you have concluded on is based solely on your emotional disposition and does not take into consideration, the situation or possible problems the other person might have. The idea is not to determine whether or not you are wrong or right but rather to analyze how you are likely to process information about people and things. You actually might be right about the person.

Another situation is when you have been accused of doing something wrong and you claim that your accusers have failed to see things from your own perspective and are only interested in their own point of view.

This is a perfect example of considering things as regards context. In this case, probably because the things said are negative, you'd notice the emphasis placed on contextual understanding of actions. There is also a slight hint of the dispositional thinking occurring simultaneously.

- **The conditioning theory**: In this case, the person is likely to do things if they are tailored and conditioned to look like their own decisions instead of as a result of coercion. This is most utilized in the advertising industry where commercials, advertisements and billboards are used to convey information that would provoke positive feelings in the population of interest. They then connect such feelings to their products thus making you feel that the product would bring such a feeling into your life. Because of this, you are more likely to purchase their product, thinking all the while that your decision was an independent one.

This is usually possible because we generally perceive things based on our emotions and are more likely to buy things because they make us feel good.

- **The cognitive dissonance theory**: Based on this theory, it is assumed that people tend to aim for consistency in their thoughts, attitudes and decisions. This is the reason why most people create principles which they strive to follow. Most people also seem intent on reconciling the contradictions as much as they can until they feel comfortable. I would give two examples on this.

Example 1

You have a very strong and deep-rooted need for canned food, either due to the laziness of having to cook meals or the frustrations at having to wait in queues for food. Then you are told that such canned meals could lead to cancer and you definitely don't want to have cancer. But you also don't want to stop eating canned food. So, instead of stopping with the habit, you comfort yourself that millions of people like you have the same habit and would never have cancer.

The cancer theory might be untrue but your eagerness to dispute the fact or at least to make the consequences seem less severe is your own way of changing your mind or at least making the facts you have just learned seem less important or true. This is one of the ways of dealing with cognitive dissonance theory.

Example 2

Imagine a criminal with a conscience. This is probably hard to imagine but they do exist. In such a situation, his or her criminal tendencies are clashing with their tender hearts and causing a bit of discomfort. Such a person is very likely dealing with his/ her problems by giving in to the rationale that a criminal and wealthy life far outweighs the benefits of having a clean conscience or good heart.

Again, I am refraining from judging whether such a rationale is sound but am more focused on the fact that the person seems to give in to a rationale that overlaps with the general aim of most people to deal with his discomfort. This is another way of dealing with the cognitive dissonance.

- **The judgement theory:** This one is very simple to grasp. It simply proposes that when faced with a new piece of information or idea a person's reaction is more or less dependent on the way he/she currently feels on the topic. What this means is that were likely to accept something that resonates with our current belief, reject something that doesn't fit in with our beliefs, or stay indifferent to something never previously considered.

  Therefore, when attempting to persuade a person, it is better to first determine their views on the topic to gauge whether or not you'd be successful and if your effort would eventually be worth it.
- **Inoculation theory:** The inoculation theory supports the view that even if previously uninterested in two points of view, once argued for, you are likely to pick the dominant point of view and stick with it. Here is an example of what I mean.

You have never watched a game of soccer in your life but one day you are relaxing on the beach and happen to find yourself stuck between two diehard soccer fans, who support rival teams. An argument begins about whose team is better and more dominant and they both turn to you, presenting their points like you are s seasoned fan and after some time ask you to judge on who's better. You obviously would pick the person with the better argument so as not to betray your own lack of knowledge on the subject. If in future another individual was to pose a question to you, inquiring as to which of those two teams is better, you'd probably find yourself arguing in favor of the choice you made then, maybe even with some of the same points that were used then.

This is the power of inoculations, the most powerful initial idea always takes root first.

- **Narrative persuasion theory:** From experience, I think we would all accept that stories have a more enhanced effect on perception and opinions than abstract advice. The attitudes and opinions of people towards objects and others tend to change when they are told compelling stories of such subjects.

The theory simply attempts to explain the heightened effect can have on people if utilized properly. In this, the listener feels transported and this greatly affects their perception of events, making them more pronounced and vivid than they might have been if they had been expressed ordinarily and abstractly.

The Psychological Perspective

Ordinarily, persuading people would be difficult without the ability to properly organize and present an argument. But if inexperience in any or both of this is coupled with an inability to gauge and understand moods and stances, your task would be made many times more likely to fail.

The ability to instantly sense and recognize a person's stance on an issue is difficult, not to talk of performing the same trick on an audience. Because of this difficulty, most speakers who are attempting to introduce people to a new point of view always tend to ask questions that would enable them gauge the stance of the audience before moving on with their presentation.

Immediately after asking such questions, they usually watch out for visible reactions from members of the audience, maybe a smile to indicate a previous knowledge of the topic, sitting up to indicate interest, turning away or sighing to indicate disagreement or boredom or even a person willing to answer. These simple markers give you an idea as to how your message may be received and would help you map out a strategy of approach. It is also an effective tool as people tend to express themselves more sincerely when they do not feel particularly in the spotlight. So, if you are unsure, do not refrain from asking a few surface questions to test the waters or more aptly, to feel out the crowd.

It should also be noted that many people might give a negative reaction to one-on-one persuasion and would start arguments to further their points. The moment you realize that your attempt to persuade a particular person has deteriorated into an argument, it is advisable for you to walk away. Very few arguments occurring outside law courts ever get settled. Engaging in one would be fruitless and time consuming. That time is better spent elsewhere.

I stated earlier that manipulation is similar to persuasion in that both aim to change opinions, attitudes and actions from what they might have been to whatever you prefer and I had also stated that they differ from one another in that, persuasion is a more direct form of securing the change you desire, while manipulation requires you to operate in secret using emotional exploitation. Now, I would like to expatiate on the relationship between manipulation and persuasion or rather how persuasion can be adopted as a tool for manipulators.

This is not rocket science and needs only a simple alteration in approach to persuasion. It would require you to couple the ability to make compelling, irrefutable arguments with your ability to recognize emotional markers. Once both are in sync, you are ready to move. But why this two? The answer to that is rather simple. If you recognize an emotion to be dominant in the target and fell the need to convince, he or she to do something without outright manipulation, most likely due to the presence of friends and family, wouldn't it be better to play on such an emotion and use it as a leverage or platform with which you propel your point of view rather than just riding in without a strategy.

This is why persuasion makes manipulation look humane and might even reduce the noticeability of your ploy. It enables the manipulator, you, to touch on the emotions of a target for a reaction, but instead of making your telling moves under a shroud all the time, you adopt clever arguments and let them do the convincing for you. The trick however, is to always get the emotion right.

Chapter 6: Persuasion: The Practical

focusing on the definition, its differences and similarities with manipulation as well as their relationship and how they could be adapted to work to your benefit as a manipulator. Other than that, the means by which the human mind absorbs and relates to new information and facts was also discussed. Now, I wish to approach how the theories of information absorption can be used to your advantage in real life situations. I want to give you practical tips on how to persuade people to do your bidding effectively.

Putting The Theories Into Practice

The theories from the previous chapter were very explanatory regarding how people are most likely to relate with information but said very little about how to take advantage of their tendencies. This should give more detailed tips and tactics as to how the theories can be used maximally in real life situations as well as the groups of people most likely to possess each attribute.

- **Use of the attribution theory:** This theory manifests in all people but is more noticeable in pseudo manipulators or arrogant people. Such people are less likely to ever accept being wrong and are more likely to blame it on perspective instead. Here is an example on hoe to deal with such people.

  Your target is a pseudo manipulator, one who likes to feel in control and powerful, and the roles in the relationship are already well defined. If on a given occasion such a person were to shut down your views in a bid to bully you into submission. You could use such an opportunity to play for something you need. Firstly, you have to avoid arguing your point for too long or too strongly. Always put up a little resistance to emphasize their power over you. Once he/she has lapsed into the role you want for them, ask them for tips on how to do what they want from you. Be sure to keep them talking, constantly asking questions and subtly driving the conversation towards your need. When they are at the their most vulnerable, they would be ready to do anything just to keep emphasizing their power.

The thing about such targets is that they are convinced of their powers over you and believe themselves to be infinitely smarter. People who think themselves smart love nothing more than giving lectures, in which your only role is to listen and ask more questions. Once you have got them talking for an extended period, proceed to move them in your direction of interest and when they appear to feel at their most powerful, they are likely to grant it without much consideration, much like the kings of old.

- **Use of the conditioning theory:** In a real-life situation, this theory involves using your wit and humor to flatter the target into believing whatever you want them to. It also makes them more likely to consider your suggestions. This follows the general principle that you would aim to acquire more of what pleases you and in this case who. A typical example is the confident guy who prides himself on being able to pick up a different girl every night. How does he do it? He simply wows and impresses them with a combination of humor, wit, an interesting conversation and a smoothness and style that is very difficult to recreate. He basically makes them feel good for five minutes at the bar and they believe he would make them feel equally as good for the entire night and therefore, happily follow him out. Though this works on almost everyone, naïve people are bound to be more success.

- **Use of the cognitive dissonance theory:** this is a generally difficult theory to use because, the onus is usually on the targets to make all the difference on their lives. But, if properly played, and you act as the adviser and close friend who gives the alternative idea or compromise that helps them deal with their dissonance, it makes you a sort of confidante. This gives you a choice position in their lives as from their point of view, you understand them more than any other person. This is, however, the sort of relationship that must be cultivated for a period of time before making your move.

- **Use of the judgement theory:** People rich in self-confidence, arrogant and who consider themselves smarter than most tend not to listen to or take into consideration arguments of other that are contradictory to their own views. If such people are to be persuaded, the new opinions they are to be inoculated with have to be similar to their previous ones or else all hopes would of persuading them would be impossible.

If you are to ever convince them that what they believe is wrong or inferior to yours, you need to make it feel that acceptance is their idea and not a necessity. The first step would be to pander to them, to defer slightly to their intelligence. Next, you draw similarities between your idea and theirs. When it comes to convincing, you are better served by an indirect approach where you ask questions and wait for them to answer, before gently expressing your objections, making sure to always be gentle and let their thought processes do the job of convincing them. It could be a change of opinion or a need to persuade them that a course of action better serves their interests, this method is sure to soften them up better than arguing with them.

Consider that friend who sees himself or herself as an authority on every subject regardless of how little knowledge they actually possess on the issue and remember how such people almost never back out of arguments but instead keep going at it till the environment of the discussion becomes toxic.

We have all had this kind of friend and the mistake of arguing with them even makes it harder for them to ever change their views. This is because, once they have taken a public stance an opinion, it is difficult for them to ever take another or even act against what they have supported, even if they later see more sense in your own view. This is because, going back on their belief is against their sense of pride and their ego. Thus, persuading such people is better done in private, if anything, because it gives you a chance to try again if you fail the first time. It also gives them a chance to adopt your idea in public without looking weak or stupid.

- **Use of the inoculation theory:** This is easy to utilize because almost everyone is susceptible to this. The key is making sure the person as no previous beliefs or opinions on the issue at hand. That is the only criterion. Once you are sure of this, you explain to them the advantages of your views. Never forget to also share the disadvantages but do this in a way that it doesn't affect the message you want them to have. The reason why the disadvantages must be made clear is that if they associate what you have explained to them with lies later along the line, they are very likely to change their views as a whole. So, if you need such people for the long term, make sure they have the full gist. Always emphasize the advantages and play down the disadvantages but never conceal them. This is as such, less a matter of persuading a person as it is initiating belief in them. For this reason, knowledge and utilization of this theory could be very powerful in the right situations. Such a situation is when you find yourself pitching a unique and previously utilized business idea in a meeting or when trying to preach a new doctrine, be it religious, academic or technological.

- **Use of the narrative persuasion theory:** The power of stories is well known. If you doubt it, all you have to do is think about how evangelists and religious clerics preach their messages. Are you getting the idea now? Though I should probably say that these clerics are probably among the most trained persons in the art of persuasion Because at one point they make use of so many theories of persuasion, constantly changing their tactics to better fit your fears and worries. But, enough with the clerics. The narrative persuasion theory is perhaps the most effective at persuading people because it involves giving them a story, a character that they could relate to and then relying on that story to do your convincing. Such a story might be true or if you are very talented, made up.

It really doesn't matter as long as you can get them to listen. It might not work every time when used alone but if you were to mix it up with other theories, just like the clerics, the chances of success are better.

Other Techniques Of Persuasion

Persuasion, like manipulation, possesses guidelines on how best to achieve your aim. These guidelines could be treated as strategies or tactics and would increase your chances of success the more you get used to them. The faster, the better.

- **Use of force:** The use of force or aggression could be effective or not and more often than not, it is a win or nothing tactic. It involves not a lot of coaxing but a lot of demanding and as such, if the person or audience don't dig the vibe, there is no other means of retreating. It usually involves use of statements that sound threatening and would most likely be a good fit for dealing with people with low self confidence and sense of self-worth. Also note that if the idea is to impress friends and family of your target, it would be better if this tactic were used in private beyond the hearing or view of other parties as it could easily be perceived as bullying.

- **Commitment and consistency:** These are highly respected values in the minds of most people in all walks of life. When coupled with a little bit of success, it could be very effective if not the most effective means of persuasion. If you want someone to believe your way is gold and your opinions are equally as rich, there is no better way than providing an example of their successes. In most cases, the best example is usually yourself. Showing commitment to your ideals and consistently applying them successfully tends to convince people of their truthfulness. It eliminates the need for you to continue arguing your points regularly, instead let them persuade themselves that following your example is the right thing. It would be like seeing a successful person and emulating them in the hopes that you'd achieve their level of success the same way. We all do it, so why not use it to our advantage when dealing with others.

Another angle to this, could be to get the target to commit themselves to promises or writing. This would be useful because most people care about reputations and rarely want to be seeing going back on their words. While this second angle would be an effective tool on arrogant people and pseudo manipulator, the first method is more likely to work for people lacking in confidence and self-esteem.

- **Social influence:** Social influence could manifest in one of two ways. It could be positive or negative. Positive influence would point to the need for one to follow the convention or approach that is the most common around him/her or among friends. The negative influence, on the other hand deals with the tendency of people to act against the norm. The influence that is expressed is usually deep rooted and expresses itself in more than one fact of the target's life. Once the targets tendency has been established, you could move to surround the person only with people who possess the approach that would produce the result you desire. This method is also applicable to people with a low sense of self-esteem and confidence.

- **Action by reciprocity:** reciprocity generally means the need or tendency to give back when you are given something. You are probably wondering how this affects persuasion, right? This is straightforward. Giving something creates the need in the target to give back. This in turn is a weakness that makes the target more susceptible to catering to a need that they otherwise could have overlooked. This is also applicable to arrogant people as well as those who possess altruistic dispositions. An empathetic person is also likely to fall for such a ruse. This could also be used or claimed to be used subliminally, as most times you need not even state the need verbally or outrightly but instead subtly imply to its absence.

- **Use of authority or sternness:** If the target is a naïve person or one who is lacking in decisiveness or assertiveness, this is the ideal method of approach. This is for people who are prone to listening to other people's opinions and taking it for the truth, especially when they consider the person to be more of an authority on the subject than they are. It would also help if they consider your views trustworthy and knowledgeable. This is the method of choice when dealing with a new or junior colleague or at least someone who is new to an environment and is not yet well versed in how things operate. However, treating such people could also be counterproductive, causing them to view you in a negative light.

- **Taking advantage of love:** It might be a simple crush or a big attraction, but people almost always say yes to people they like and feel something positive for. So, if you have a target that you feel is attracted to you, play their feelings to your advantage and ask for whatever you want, just be careful to give a little back and do not overdo it. If the person is emotionally dependent on you, your luck is strong because they are even less likely to utter a word for fear of losing you to another. The best part is that they never realize that such is happening, as it is a very natural reaction.
- **Leveraging your trust and integrity:** if you are generally acknowledged to be trustworthy, you are more likely to be believed. This could be done by smartly showing off your impeccable reputation, if you have one, while avoiding the line of arrogance. That could spoil the effect. Another way to use this tactic is to put your character in the spotlight, if you have a good one, and making sure to back up your every point with a vow of assurance in its trustworthiness.

  The last is to give a sense of expertise. Show that you possess more knowledge than they do and when added to your reputation and character, you have a cocktail of persuasion that even the most steadfast of non-believers would reconsider. It is also likely to work on naïve people and people who consider themselves intellectual.
- **Making use of sympathy and empathy:** These two emotions can easily be manipulated because they usually convey on their owners, a sense of innocence and docility that can be used against them. With the right words and gestures, you should be able to convince such people of anything. For a more advanced effect, make use of stories as such people are also prone to following the narrative transportation theory and the combination of these two factors make them better candidates to believe than most.

Reverse Psychology

Reverse psychology is a technique of persuasion where a speaker or person utilizes a behavior or idea that is contradictory to that which he wants to occur. The user of this technique does or asks for the opposite of what they actually require of the target, encouraging the target to do as they wish.

This works on people who make a habit of resisting authority. If tried on people who are more agreeable, they might and would probably do as you have asked. For this reason, they do not make good candidates or targets for reverse psychology to be used upon.

However, even when used with resistant people, reverse psychology should be used as subtly as possible because no one enjoys or likes being manipulated and as such, if they recognize what you are doing, it is likely you would not achieve much with them. An example of the use of reverse psychology is advising someone to do something when you know that the very idea of the advice infuriates him/her and would probably push them towards doing the opposite. The idea is usually to establish the idea you actually want them to absorb then play it up subtly to become tempting, before changing tack and arguing against it. Immediately after this, you push them to make a decision and that's all. It is likely that they would go with it because other than the fact that they would want to resist the advice, it is also the idea that they were exposed to first. It is not necessary to take such steps if you know the person well enough to understand what they like, dislike and how they would react in given situations.

Remember To Always Analyze Before Making Your Move

The reason why most people fail in persuading people into a line of action is that they fail to grasp what is necessary for their success and if they do, they fail to take it all into consideration. It is for this same reason that persuading strangers is more difficult than persuading people you are closer to. Because if you were to ignore a person's emotional disposition and shelf their possible reactions, it would be the same as approaching a stranger. To really succeed at persuasion, most times you might need to adopt maybe a dominant, authoritative attitude or a more reserved one.

When being authoritative, you have to give off a vibe of knowledgeability and confidence. You must convince the person that you know what you are speaking about, while emphasizing their own knowledge. There is a loophole here. If this is tried on a resistant person, he or she is likely to do the opposite of what you advise and thus fall a victim of reverse psychology. You see that knowledge of the person is important in determining the best technique for persuasion for without it, you would be charging blindly.

You should also avoid using reverse psychology very often as such misuse could expose your tricks and make the target more immune to your ministrations. It could be particularly damaging to relationships and you do not want this, unless that in itself is your goal. If you are to use reverse psychology, always remember to stay smart and stay calm. Do not let your emotions control you but, just like in manipulation, control your emotions.

Persuasion is an art that all socially influential people crave possession of. This is because the ability to make people do as you wish and while you can directly manipulate individuals, it becomes trickier when dealing with groups of people. But if you were to master this art, your power and influence would benefit greatly.

Chapter 7: Common Manipulation Techniques

At a point in our life, and at least once daily for most, we resort to manipulation to get what we want. It could be a little lie to get out of a tight spot or harmless flattery to get yourself a choice seat but it is manipulation. So, stop believing that manipulation is an art reserved for only the evilest of people, everyone does it so it's simply better to get very good at it. Though it is better to look out for some traits that predispose some to manipulation more than others, it doesn't mean that people without such traits can't be played.

I have previously elaborated on such traits as well as other means of gaining control over people but it's time to approach the real topic of discussion, how to manipulate people.

Lying

This is the most popular of all manipulation techniques. On its own, lying is simply misinforming the target or at the most, concealing information from the target but when done with a view to controlling people, it becomes a pretty powerful weapon. Consider lying as a tool to soften up a target that has until that moment proven too strong. Lying in this way would require one to betray the very intent of conventional lying because in this case, you are not trying to misinform or conceal but rather to confuse.

If you are to succeed at this, your lies need to be believable and contradictory at first. At the beginning of such a ploy, it is necessary for your lies to constantly bounce of each other, creating a means through which you could sow seeds of confusion in someone who is usually sure of themselves.

Consider lying to a partner about a past relationship. Then in a later discussion on a similar topic, drop a previously thought of slip-up that contradicts the first experiences you shared with them. The target might not notice this at first and may require a few more similar lies before the inconsistencies start to call their attention but when it does, instead of defending yourself, clam up and play the victim. Tell a sob story about emotional pain and all of that; share with them the reason for your lies. The stories and reasons might be fictitious, but the more realistic the better. So, be sure to think everything through first.

In this sort of scenario, the initial contradicting lies are needed to throw a seemingly strong person off balance. There is nothing like a perfect person or a truly balanced person and, as such, regardless of how strong we might seem on the outside, we all have weaknesses and there is no better way to start the process of exposing someone's emotional vulnerabilities than forcing them to instigate a heart to heart moment or discussion. If you were to try creating such a moment on your own, the target would still be likely to stay closed. However, if such a discussion is their idea, whatever barriers they possessed, they would have brought down by themselves. That is the goal with this lie.

It puts you in a position to change the narrative. In a situation in which the power was previously balanced in most of your relations, making yourself seem weak or vulnerable could put the target in an uncomfortable position and force them into opening up to adapt to their new role. Just be sure to keep any contradictory lies out of your final story. While this might not bring you much in terms of favors, having them belief you opened up on some deep secret to them strengthens their attachment. they feel a stronger bond has been formed. This trick is likely to work on people who are emotionally secure and need to believe you are really open with them before they can open up.

Punishment

When I say punishment, I do not mean physical abuse or violence. No, I mean resorting to tactics like the silent treatment, nagging, shouting or mood swings. I know you are probably thinking how any of these behaviors could get you any control but if you learn to selectively release such emotions and actions at the right time, they could exert just the right effect on the target.

The silent treatment for example could be used to put the right person in a state of wanting to please you. This treatment is a popular one for manipulators when dealing with assertive people as well as people with low self-confidence. In such case, you create a fictional quarrel in your head that need not have happened in reality. All it needs to be is believable and offensive from your perspective. Then follow through with the silent treatment. When the target gets desperate to get you back to your former self, drop the act and ask for whatever you wish for. This is a direct technique that might not always work but for a beginner, it is worth a try and for an expert, if partnered with the right set of skills and ploys, its chances of success become better.

Remember when you were little and your parents tried keeping you away from the candy or cookie jar and instead of throwing a tantrum and crying, you just stalked back to your room, threw the sheets over your head and refused to talk to anybody. You wait for hours determined not to make the first move and, later at night your parents come into the room, bearing gifts and treats and maybe even the promise of a trip you want.

Not all children did this but most did and yes, children manipulate too. They might not recognize it for what it is but they actually do it and since it works, they keep resorting to it again and again. The best thing about such a ploy is at the exact instance during which it occurs, the target believes that they are doing the right thing to keep you happy and keep the relationship from dying.

If nagging were to be the strategy of choice for you. Be sure the target is either one who lacks assertiveness or one who is eager to please because such people are likely to react favorably to nagging. Let's say you want something badly, all you have to do is keep asking and asking until they give in. Due to their lack of assertiveness, through all the asking, they would probably never give you an outright no for an answer and if it is a target who is always eager to please, he or she would have begun considering the pros and cons from the second time you ask and with just a little extra push, they would cave.

Mood swings are another very effective strategy in unbalancing a target. They are just more negative than lying and if utilized, care has to be taken to avoid dwelling too much or for too long on negative emotions such as anger. rather, it would be better to spend more time in a neutral state of boredom or indifference. The trick behind utilizing mood swings is to make your target associate some actions of theirs with particular moods of yours. This would give them an idea about what you like and dislike without you uttering a word. It is thus, advised to use this tactic alongside a more reserved attitude.

Imagine your roommate tends to leave their dishes undone after a meal, you do something drastic like throwing such plates in the trash and then refrain from talking much about it for that night but when you wake the next morning, you adopt a lighthearted demeanor and refuse to lower the smile regardless of what he or she does.

The next time, your roommate invites someone over without informing you and you act in a similar way. You never let your reactions slip over into the next day and other than when the target does something you find offensive, never react in such a way. Also, make sure that you do this only rarely.

Depending on the type of person your roommates is he or she would react differently. If the person is naive or is lacking in self-esteem, they would pander to you and fail to repeat whatever it is you reacted to but if the person is insensitive, your reactions would probably not do the trick and you would have to resort to another tactic.

Sarcasm and flattery

How To Influence People

While other techniques mentioned earlier have dealt with manipulation using actions and acting, if you are good with words, this is a more likely weapon for you. The power of words is often underexaggerated in favor of actions. However, if mastered, they could be just as useful if not more.

Sarcasm and flattery are two slightly contrasting techniques that could be used to control the actions and opinions of people. They are usually most effective on someone who lacks self-esteem. Such a person is likely to believe most negative and positive things you say about them and start working to please you. Because of this, you could use sarcasm to deliver well planned putdowns whenever such a person offends you, only to resort to flattery to increase their confidence. Such polarity on such a week mind means they would cling to you for the compliments and flattery and would start doing things only to please you even if it goes against their own needs.

The applications of sarcasm and flattery lose all or at least most of their effectiveness if they are blatantly employed. To avoid these you must understand the need for subtlety. In the case of sarcasm, the very idea is for you to be blatant in your execution while subtly hiding your goal. You must make whatever comment you deem fit without making the target feel as if you are directing them towards a particular line of action. Failing at this could have the alternate effect of making them immune to you.

When you were young, you probably associated bullies with violence, shoving people into lockers and all but you should be able to point out that person who always alternated in behavior, showing you his or her good parts on one day, only to switch it up the next. The person would have been so polarizing that people were often confused about whether they loathed or loved him or her and with time would start to find that they hovered around such people, trying to cater to their every need. Do you recognize them now? You probably had a few in your high school and most times they were really popular.

Two of the most effective tactics employed by those people were sarcasm and flattery. With subtle swipes of their tongues they could play down your happiest moment or your biggest achievement to be something worthless and in the next, they could make one of your more ordinary actions seem spectacular. As much as they hurt your feelings, you'd still find yourself doing things they would find pleasing whenever they were around.

This might have happened to you and it might not have but the very fact that it happened to some speaks volumes of the effectiveness of such tactics. So, never forget to destabilize a mark using sarcasm and flattery. Another advantage of these two techniques is that they keep you from having to resort to trickier aggressive or abusive techniques when slight words and gestures would do the trick perfectly.

Isolation

This is mostly a secondary tactic used to make sure no external forces mess with your manipulation. The presence of family and friends around the target provide an extra level of insulation or protection around the target as such people tend to call the target back on some of their actions when they get suspicious. Their presence there, whispering into the ear of the mark thus creates another source of influence, besides yours, whose sole purpose is to thwart your influence.

Whenever you get the target to fulfil a need for you such people would call he/she back and try to expose how you are manipulating them and that puts the ploy you have implemented in jeopardy.

On its own, isolation is not that effective but it is worth noting that in the absence of friends and family alike, the target starts to look onto you as their only source of advice, comfort, love, help etc. In other words, they become completely dependent on you emotionally and this heightens the level of control you possess over them. This in turn makes them easier to influence.

Guilt tripping and love bombing

These two are a very common duo used by manipulators but that doesn't in any way affect their effectiveness. Guilt tripping is when you manipulate your targets reactions making them feel guilty about doing particular things simply by playing on their emotional vulnerabilities. Naturally, guilt is a very uncomfortable feeling which most people strive to eliminate. This need to eliminate their guilt after an incident is what you should aim to take advantage of. Since such chances might be few and far between, the initiative to create situations that give you a platform on which you could leverage a person's guilt against them is on you. In such a case, the understanding of your targets emotions and what makes them tick comes into play. You need to know how you can make them feel guilty so as to take advantage of them and their guilt.

Consider a situation in which a partner or girlfriend refuses to accompany you to a company gathering. If the gathering is not important to you, you could clam up and use a mood swing to leverage them for something that is. But if you consider the gathering too important to miss or you need a plus one to impress a particular attendee and your partner is refusing. You could play the guilt card, making them feel selfish and unkind for not considering your needs. You would make yourself the victim, putting your partner in an awkward position where they feel like they are depriving you of something you need for their own selfish reason. When this is used on less assertive people or people lacking in self-confidence, the result is usually stunning as more often than not they end up doing exactly what you want. They might even outperform your expectations simply because of their need to eliminate the feelings of guilt you have created in them.

Using such a tactic, you rile up someone that loves or is attached to you by telling them and claiming that they do not care or are too selfish in the way they treat you. This would keep an emotionally vulnerable person in check, making them see you as the victim of their actions a rather than the other way around. They would then be eager to prove your claims wrong, thus, increasing in them the need to please.

Love bombing, on the other hand, is a technique in which you continuously and over an extended period of time shower a person with love, impressing them with charm while getting whatever you want from them. This is usually much difficult to tell apart from real love and that's what makes the mark even more vulnerable. Love bombing is effective on almost everyone because as humans we all love to feel good and this need drives our selection of the people we hang out with. If someone makes us feel loved and cared for, we impulsively strive to spend more time with them. This would also mean that the target would feel more inclined to satisfy your need in order to maintain his or her happiness. However, like most tactics, the effect of love bombing is more pronounced in some character types. What this means is that, depending on the level of love bombing you expose a target to, some would see it is as a result of you trying to be nice and would consider you a good friend while other would see your actions as more and would consider you as more than a friend.

Individually, love bombing and guilt tripping are effective but when combined they are devastating. I am yet to explain reinforcement but the effect they produce is quite similar. To achieve such an effect, you should probably expose the target to your loving and charming side. Make the effect of your love felt then when the moment is right, you withdraw it and leave the target craving for it. The next step is to up the ante by making them feel guilty about your withdrawal. You make them feel like your current mood and state is their fault and when you feel that they are ripe and ready to accommodate your whims and needs, you slowly slip back into the role of loving and caring for them.

Most of the time, this works and its success is because every time you put both ploys in play, you create a sort of hypersensitivity to your needs and wants in the target. You get them into a state a where all they want to do is return to the period of time when all you did was love them and charm them.

You might also resort to completely playing the victim just to make the target more uncomfortable and guiltier, softening them up for whatever it is that you actually want of them.

This is the technique used by con men and women who want to take advantage of vulnerable people and make some wealth for themselves in the process. They inveigle their way into the lives of such people and then love-bomb them to the point where, the target cannot imagine an extended period of time without them and would, for that reason alone, do anything to keep them happy. Whenever they fail to get their way, they would then resort to guilt tripping in order to bring the target back into a state of mind in which their major thought would be on pleasing them. It might seem odd and unbelievable but if you think about it long enough, you'd realize that these two are the most used techniques by gold diggers and emotional swindlers.

Reinforcement

This technique is easy to understand but hard to actually apply and as such is better learnt by trial and error. In this ploy, you provide the target with whatever he or she wants, be it money, gifts, sex or companionship, provided it is within your capability. And after the person grows accustomed to having what you give them, you begin the process of constantly withdrawing and providing them with these, constantly keeping them on their toes and making them vulnerable with you.

The major trick here is figuring out what the target wants, what makes them tick or what most tickles their ego. You have to identify that weakness that everyone has and reinforce it. It might be praise and recognition the person desires, give it to them. It might be money and gifts, give it to them. It might be sex or prestige, give it to them. But whenever you feel they are not conforming to your whims or are not taking care of your needs or are even daring to take you for granted, withdraw all that you have given to them and in a bid to get it all back, they would come groveling and begging. After the first time, they would probably learn to satisfy your every want if they don't want you withdrawing your reinforcement.

For example, there is at least a smidgen of materialism in all of us and this can be taken advantage of. If you meet a lady whose weakness lies in her love of material possessions and you have the money to spend, you are in luck. All you have to do is charm her, take her on a few shopping trips, spend your money on her and basically reinforce her love of material things. Upon every reinforcement, try upping the ante on the things you ask of her. You could start with insisting she spend more time with you, insisting she accompany you to any event you wish and with time you could try asking her or commanding her to stay over whenever you like. To keep up the supply of riches, love for which you have reinforced in her, she would most likely conform to your needs or at least beg for a reprieve rather than reject you. But if she seems to take your kindness for granted, kick her to the curb and withdraw your reinforcement. She is likely to come back hat in hand, apologizing for her behavior and eager to please.

Not to restrict this to only your love life, this technique could also be applied to almost any setting, including business, family relationships and any case in general provided there exist a means by which you reinforce the individual or group involved. If you think about it, you would notice that there really is little difference between this and parents who threaten to ground you and take away your freedom unless you behave as they wish or business men who pull out of deals with established customers in the hope of pushing them into making desperate, unfavorable deals that would benefit them.

In the case of the parents, they have reinforced your love of freedom by allowing you do the things you like most of the time. This, when coupled with our inherent need to be free, makes us eager to please them anytime they threaten to take that freedom away. Couple the love for freedom with the fact that they are your providers of everything you need and you would see that they have quite the hold on you.

As I implied earlier, manipulation is rife in the world and silently hoping for an ideal world in which it doesn't exist would make no difference. It is better you wizen up and get better at it than other before you are taken on a ride.

I left this as the last technique on my list because there is a possibility or rather, an inevitable reaction that you always have to take into consideration when dealing with people. This is ingratitude or sometimes boredom. People tend to take for granted things they can have all the time and over a long period of time, they are bound to get bored. To avoid this, you would need to be very good at utilizing multiple techniques at various times on the same target.

This ingratitude or boredom is most likely to occur when reinforcement is used and to counter this reaction you must understand that whatever you are reinforcing in the target could make them take you for granted. Because of this, you must always be ready to withdraw your reinforcement not only when they misbehave but also when you like to. This sounds mean and selfish and it actually is, but you need to know that for reinforcement to work, you need to be selfish. You have to make the target see your needs as being more important than theirs and to successfully do this, selfishness is necessary. The target needs to know that your efforts at making them feel good come at a price and the price is anything you want in return. Thus, being nice doesn't cut it here; you need to be mean sometimes to truly make it work for you.

Manipulation Is Not Always For The Faint Hearted

Manipulation is not always wrong, nor is it always right but one thing that can be agreed upon is that it leaves an effect on both the user and the target. Depending on how manipulation was used, the effect might be positive or negative. Manipulation is usually used as a means of harming, subduing or using a person usually in a way that benefits the manipulator mostly at the expense of the target. The negative effects of manipulation are not experienced by the victim alone and in most cases, the users are not aware of the negative effects their behavior is having on their lives and, thus, become victims of their own manipulation. One of the problems of manipulation is the transfer or possession of power.

Power is naturally very addictive and very corrupting and so when faced with the question of what to use the power you have over people for, people tend to think about their selfish needs and how to make them happen. The idea of having power over a group of people or person is tempting and when such power is gotten it can lead to complete subordination and even abuse. While that is an effect on the victim, the user of such power might also become dependent on it thus making it difficult for them to have any sort of relationship with anybody unless they have power to exert. This can be damaging, both psychologically and emotionally, in the long run.

Chapter 8: Mastering The Art Of Subtlety-Do Not Be Blatant

If manipulation isn't subtle, it probably wouldn't be effective. The very idea of manipulation thrives on the ability to subtly plant ideas, thoughts and opinions in the mind of the target and frame it in such a way that they believe that such ideas are the best they could come up with or the right thing to do.

Subtlety is necessary because the target has to feel that your every action is natural and actually not intended to influence them. This would mean that you first have to reduce the frequency with which you manipulate them. Manipulating them would mean reacting regularly in a negative way to what they do. This might seem unnatural to the target and could even lead them into believing that you are always trying to push on their buttons which, by the way, you are. The ability to be subtle is as important as the ability to read emotions because subtlety makes your knowledge of their emotions and reactions remain unknown to them.

Being blatant in the way you manipulate a person would also draw the attention of other people such as friends and family and, in all honesty, there is hardly a better way to put your manipulation of a target in jeopardy than exposing them to the influence of their family and friends. The simple secret to being subtle is to keep your judgements to yourself and keep your actions and reactions as cool and as undetectable as possible.

The Cautious Approach Is Always Best

Regardless of how vulnerable a target might seem or how susceptible to manipulation they might look from a distance, it is necessary for you to approach the idea of manipulating a person cautiously. It isn't ever something to jump into just because of the possibility that the manipulation could be successful.

Cautiousness has to extend to all areas of the manipulation, from the planning to the approach and everything in between. This is especially important when dealing with strangers or people with whom you haven't spent that much time with. The emotions of such people are usually difficult to follow, even for the experts, and as such it is better to proceed with utmost caution at first and consolidate on the little progress you make.

The same thing applies when dealing with people you know because even though the chances of you getting it wrong is very slim, it still exists and for this reason you have to consider your actions before going on with them otherwise you risk destroying your relationships.

Another problem with throwing caution to the wind is that it exposes your tactics and your goal to the target. While some people might just cut you loose and move on with their lives, others might feel the need to expose you to a dose of your own medicine. Such people would probably try to manipulate you in return with a view at causing you pain. So, if the need to succeed does not make you cautious, maybe thinking about your own well-being does the trick.

A Flimsy Ploy Is Ineffective

Other than the ability to actually go through with the manipulation, another thing to pay attention to is the solidity of the ploy. This consists of details such as the rightness of the strategy to be utilized as regards the emotional and psychological disposition of the target as well as the situation in which you find yourself in.

The technique applied always has to seem like a natural reaction to whatever situation you find yourself in. If the reaction is unnatural, the ploy might still work out but if looked at closely, what you are doing would become more visible to the target and more so to outsiders who lack the emotional dependence the target has for you.

For this reason, no matter who the target is or how long the relationship has been going on for, you always need to make sure that the manipulation is foolproof and that no one is the wiser to your plans.

Scouting out the right target and putting the right approach into play would be useless if the general ploy is easily seen through. The ploy has to consist of you yourself, the image you are portraying to the target, how the role you are playing interacts with your actions and most importantly, the fluidity of the entire ploy. If any of this is found lacking or for some reason, the various elements are found to be out of sync with one another, the chances of success reduce considerably.

Never Get Ahead Of Yourself

The ability to keep yourself on track and put your mind to the task even when things are going well for you is an important attribute in every facet of life. Regardless of how well the relationship might be for you at a particular time or how much the manipulation is serving your interests, never ever lose track of yourself.

A loss of concentration could manifest in many ways. It could be a tendency for you to lose hold of your target, a need to avoid subtlety or the urge to fast-track a ploy. Any of these is risky as it exposes you to a better chance of failure, which in turn could lead to a complete breakdown of your plan. You must always stay alert to your surroundings and the reactions of your target to them. You must never fail to recognize how a situation affects a target or else you risk losing them prematurely.

Never Go All Out Unless...

Subtlety is a rule most manipulators always conform to. The ones who choose to not obey this are often less successful and when they succeed, their success is usually short-lived. We have established the need for secrecy and subtlety but there are times when being subtle is disadvantageous or not as effective as being blatant. In these cases, you are advised to apply the needed pressure where necessary.

The ability to recognize when a situation requires more pressure than finesse as well as the best way to deliver such pressure is one garnered through experience and failure.

Situations that could call for the application of pressure are numerous but you must be able to determine if the pressure is actually necessary and how to apply it. One such situation is the need to keep a target when you feel they are slipping away.

For example, you have been working a target for a while. You have done everything by the book, maintaining isolation, staying on guard and generally looking out for any potential spoilers while getting what you want from the target. Then, in comes an old friend who is not so charmed by you. This friend goes on the attack, trying to pull the target from your clutches and you have really worked out to get to this point. You don't want to stop now. Then to bring your target back, you do something drastic like proposing marriage. This is the sort of pressure I am talking about.

In such a situation, you would agree that all other more subtle methods might and probably had already failed under such a spirited assault from the friend but instead of pulling out and walking away, you do the one thing that would express your desperation to keep the target close to you. Saying this here makes it look like showing desperation is a bad thing but from the point of view of the target, it convinces them of the truthfulness of your affection. If such a friend truly suspected of manipulation, she would have most likely used your avoidance of true commitment to prove her point and such an act would completely vilify their views and opinions in the eye of the target.

Chapter 9: Practical Uses of Manipulation

Manipulation as a tool is quite versatile as it does not particularly have any situations that it is restricted to. What this means is that, as long as people are involved in whatever you are involved in, be it a business setting, a relationship or whatever, manipulation can be used to further your agenda

Manipulation in Business

The knowledge of manipulation and persuasion is critical if you plan to avoid being drawn into office politics not of your making or if you are out to avoid being cheated or railroaded by superiors and colleagues alike. Also, in business settings, there is a need for members of the same organization or group to confirm their views with one another and influence each other to cater to the group's interests. The ability to persuade people that your point of view is best would be quite handy in such a scenario.

Sales people also need to be well versed in the arts because most times they deal with people who believe them to be swindlers and for that reason they need to manipulate the persons perception of them, creating a positive one, before they could then begin the process of persuading such a customer to try out their products. there are some informal rules to follow when practicing manipulation in such business setting.

1. Don't push the limits: when I say limits, I do not mean yours, I mean that of the people you are manipulating. One of the ways that people punish the limit is by trying to manipulate everyone very time. While this might work effectively in a relationship, in an organization, everyone watches everyone closely and being associate with a tendency to manipulate people does not do your credibility much good.

You have to be smart enough and disciplined enough to refrain from doing anything unless it is important. You have to always pick your battles well. If you overdo it and people start to view you as manipulator, they start to monitor your every move and even the most mundane of your actions become an object of intense scrutiny. Such scrutiny would make it a whole lot more difficult for you to achieve anything when it truly matters.

2. Sharpen your senses: Senses in this sense mean the ability to listen to and watch others. In a business setting, the ability to listen and perceive the disposition of others and so, when possible, say nothing, take a backseat and let others have the floor. Due to the fact that everybody in such a setting is always trying to get ahead of the next, it would be better if you could discern their strategies and goals, and there is no better way to achieve that by putting yourself in a position to hear and see everything.

3. Create a connection: Be it a customer or a colleague, you have to build a connection with them. Most people make the mistake of believing that they only need to build connections with their bosses but this line of action would only serve to paint you as your boss' stooge and alienate you from your fellow workers. on the contrary, forging a bond with both your colleagues and your bosses would make them see you as more of a bridge and less of a stooge. Another need for such a connection is the fact that you are more likely to be in the position to influence the thoughts and opinions of people when they feel they have a connection with you than if they consider you a complete stranger. This is particularly important when you are pitching an idea to others and its absence is the major reason why cold pitching is a very difficult trick to pull off.

4. Always stay neutral, when you can. in a business setting, neutrality should be your best strategy. Never take sides unless you have utmost confidence as to which side possesses more power. Taking sides early on would strip you of your flexibility and limit you to working only one angle. You must eb adept at playing both sides until you recognize which side would come out on top. The right way to maintain neutrality is to acknowledge the talents of everyone equally while also expressing real views regarding their failures. Other than strengthening your position of neutrality, such a tactic would also earn you the respect of everyone. However, like every other tactic you have to know when to apply this and this knowledge would be the difference between you successfully holding you position or even advancing in the ranks and you ailing spectacularly.

Manipulation In Relationships

Manipulation ion relationships is the one society is most sensitive about. If you manipulate in the office, most people, outsiders, would view it a s a general tactic used by many in the same situation, but manipulating in a relationship is in the eye of most, a negative marker on the character of the manipulator. Regardless of whether your intentions are pure or selfish, this opinion does not change and it is for this reason that whatever plan you have for a spouse or close friend must be done in utmost secrecy. This brings us to a previously stated point, isolation.

Isolation is one of the most important factors to be considered if you want your manipulation of a person to be successful. You must wean the target off their family and friends, establishing yourself as their confidante and emotional companion. This is because the external influence exercised by such people is capable of rivalling that which you have created and rendering your plans a waste of time.

Another thing to pay attention to is your intention. You must be disciplined, check yourself and make sure that your needs from the target do not morph into complete selfishness. You must learn to control and wield the power you possess over them with caution and with sense to avoid causing them harm. This is only possible if you think beyond your own needs and ask yourself if your need might lead to any negative consequences for the target and if so, how serious such consequences would be. Manipulation is a very powerful tool and should be treated as such.

Manipulating A Friend

Of all settings for manipulation, this is the most popular and the least suspicious or revolting. Manipulating a friend is so common, we barely pay attention to it. It usually manifests when we want to get information or something out of one another.

The best and easiest method of manipulating friends is through the use of reciprocity and compliments. Sometimes we do favors for friends because we want to but we also grant difficult favors not because we want to but because we recognize that we might need something equally as difficult to grant in the future. You do not always have to do big things, it might be a couple of smaller favors, but having them in the bag means you could leverage on reciprocity later in the future. Beware of insensitive or particularly selfish people, because they tend to not conform to reciprocity except it favors them in the moment.

The use of compliments is another way by which we unknowingly and harmlessly manipulate ourselves. The compliment might be sincere or insincere but when we give them, we recognize that they make our friends feel better about whatever it is they might have done, making them more likely to make us feel better too, whether by returning such compliments or by other means.

Offering support sort of falls under reciprocity but it is still valid as a standalone point. We might argue that offering our support to our friends in arguments and in their time of need is the right thing to do but even when we think they are wrong, we rarely ever withdraw our support. why? This is because, when we have arguments or times when we need support, we recognize the need to have someone in our corner and who better than someone who we offer unconditional support to when they need it. You can see that the manipulation is usually unintentional and harmless, but it is still a manipulation because if faced with the same choice when another person is involved, such a friend would probably do what they feel is right and not what you need. In this way, you can see that the need to reciprocate the support you showed has altered their behavior and reactions.

Seductive Manipulation

Like cleopatras manipulation of both Julius Caesar and Mark Anthony, this involves using your sexuality and possible sexual prowess as a tool in getting whatever it is you need from a target. While this is an effective method, it also doesn't last that long if you can't get the target to develop more tangible feelings for you.

The truth is that there is a limit to how long sex can hold a person down and because of this, it is better to initially play hard to get. This has the double effect of making them mistake their lust for a more potent feeling while also pushing them to impress you just to get closer to achieving their target, which is having you. The key is in the timing. You have to be able to realize when the target might be losing interest and also recognize the steps you have to take to reignite their interest. Finally, you have to know when to give in. It would be better for your ploy if you have the sexual prowess to match your games as this would make you less of a pretender and more of the real deal.

If properly played, a game of seductive manipulation could lead to real feelings and would thus make the target even more dependent on you. Everyone is susceptible to this sort of manipulation because we all crave emotional and physical relationships with others regardless of how small the urge is.

How To Properly Manipulate Strangers

Strangers are the hardest to manipulate or persuade because you usually have no idea how they think, how they process information or what makes them tick. In fact, most of the time, when you approach a stranger you find yourself following your instincts and searching for a foothold in their minds that you can leverage into a real connection. This is the smart way to go when dealing with individuals you barely know but such a method is slow and could end up being frustrating.

The alternative is quicker, riskier and used mostly by pick up artists. It is one in which you walk up to the target and impress he or she with an intoxicating mix of charm, wit and the promise of a very interesting future. This plan could fall by the wayside if your version of humor doesn't click with theirs or if your target is in the wrong state of mind for your ploy to have an effect.

Another way is to go all out and state what you want. This is rarely utilized, mostly because it betrays the very essence of manipulation; secrecy and emotional control. It is also rarely successful, so unless you are feeling lucky or the universe seems to be in your corner, don't try it.

Chapter 10: Manipulating and Scouting: The Forgotten Connection

I like to compare the game of manipulation to the hunting rituals of a predator while hunting a prey. When hunting prey, the lions of the African savannah watch their unfortunate prey - say a herd of wildebeests grazing in the distance. The lions (usually a pride) lie in wait, studying the unsuspecting prey, analyzing the herd and seeking out the weak and the vulnerable of the herd, pretty much scouting the herd. After successfully picking a target, the lions then plan a mode of attack, assigning the roles of distraction and decoys to certain individuals of the pack, some to cut off the escape routes of the prey and finally one or more to finally bring down the prey.

The manipulation game isn't too different from the scenario explained above. When scouting, the idea is not to hide or to skulk in the dark but rather to size up your target emotionally and psychologically. It is the process by which you identify the initial footholds present in their minds and how they could be used to your advantage.

Naturally, when starting the process of manipulation with a stranger, you are usually starting out blind but when you skip the scouting phase altogether, you consign yourself to starting out on the weakest possible footing, further reducing your chances of succeeding.

Watching Your Target Is Important

This is the first step and the very foundation of manipulating a target. As shown by the hunting lions, watching or studying gives you a basic info of the target helping you understand the targets habits, likes and dislikes, wants and aspirations of such target that can be exploited. Things that would prove useful in your arsenal for securing the target. A knowledge of the relevant basic info of a target reveals the weak points of such target, providing spots to be exploited to get what is needed and knowing how to trigger such target to get the required result. A good example of those weak points is the human emotions.

As humans, a considerable amount of us tend to act and make decisions under the influence of our emotions and are as a result, slaves to our emotions. Emotions make a man because they are his basest, truest reactions to a situation and most of the time we fall victim to our own emotions, expressing them without control and as such leaving us exposed to the ministrations and knowledgeable tweaking of manipulators. As earlier implied, you must always reserve extreme control over your own emotions and judge every situation logically. This helps you make the right decisions in every situation and also protects you from manipulation as you are the only one with a knowledge of your feelings.

These emotions can act as catalysts to the decision-making process of the human mind without a lot of us realizing it. For example, an altruistic person - that selfless individual who wants to do right by everyone. Such person's need to satisfy everyone can be exploited by the classic guilt trip move, by making them feel sad and unfulfilled and making them do what you want.

The knowledge gleaned from watching a target cannot be underestimated and should be of immense importance to your initial actions concerning such a target, guiding your action and words.

Establishing Trust

The importance of trust in manipulation can never be overstated. It is like the key which finally opens a door to a lost store of gems and treasures. just like without the key, you have no access to the treasures which lay inside, so can you not truly manipulate a person without gaining their trust. This is the mistake made by pseudo manipulators and you would do well not to make similar ones. They make the mistake of misjudging how much the target trusts them and as such show their hand too early. As a result, they are exposed to manipulation themselves because they then trust every one of your actions and words to be as a result of their influence.

Trust has always been an active and essential ingredient for a successful human relationship. A child trusts its parent(s) that is why he/she can follow such parent to anywhere without fear for harm. So, it is with is with the targets of manipulation, once you have secured their trust, you become infallible, your decisions are regarded to be the accurate, and your word is held in highest regard.

In some cases, this trust is easily gotten, like in the instance of the altruistic, good-willing and generally naive people. But in other cases, it is not always gotten so easily as one might have to go through various tests to finally earn that trust, but once the trust is finally earned, it is always worth the effort.

You basically have them in the palm of your hand at this level, and they are as clay in the hands of a potter in your own hands - ready to bend to whatever direction you may wish.

The subject of trust is also a critical one as trust is as easy to lose as it is hard to gain. A couple of mistakes could easily cause you to lose the hard-earned trust of a target, and trust when lost, isn't always exactly gotten back. Even if it is gotten back, it is never always in full.

Planning A Strategy Of Approach

Most of the time, for any endeavor to be successful you need a strategy. Referencing the predator/prey scenario earlier stated, a strategy is a means towards an end or ultimate result. The word strategy brings the game of chess to mind. Every smart player knows that to win, a strategy must be in place to achieve such result. If trust is the key to a den of treasures, then your strategy is your plan to avoid the uncanny traps placed around to prevent seekers from reaching the treasure. The manipulation of a target has now become like a game of chess where your every move must be tailored and aimed to getting what you want. It has become a game which for every action of the target, there should be a suitable reaction on the part of the manipulator to help get what is needed.

Since human beings can be quite dissimilar in terms of constitution, intelligence and emotional make-up, it goes without saying that one strategy cannot work for all and different strategies should be employed for different targets and different occasions. One can choose to work a target little by little, slowly but surely getting the required result or one could alternatively leave a "bait" for the target and wait patiently for the bite.

The strategy applied must take into consideration the default emotional state of the target, the level of isolation of the target, the peculiarities of the person as well as the general nature of the person. All of this are very important and neglect of anyone could lead to failure.

Follow Only What You See Or Hear

This is in a way related to the first point. Watching and studying the target would provide you with clues to exploit when working a target. These clues should be your pointers, guiding you on the next step to take or what to say next. But contrary to the first point, this is a warning. You should never try to use a clue or a feeling not present in a particular target against him/her.

As humans, we possess the tendency to judge people based on what we would do in their shoes and not based on what they have shown they would do. You have to kick out this tendency as it could mess with your reactions to the targets actions even without clouding your judgement. It makes you doubt the soundness of your judgement, pushing you to react against what you would do and feel instead of what you can observe the target doing or feeling.

Indiscriminate or excessive use of such could put you in trouble and you could ruin the whole process, causing you to start the whole process all the way from the beginning. Never forget, the idea behind a successful manipulation is determining the targets emotional state and reactions and using this to your advantage. Never let doubt creep in and spoil what is already almost done, only follow what you can see and hear and nothing else.

Conclusion

Understanding the key to manipulation and persuasion is very useful in daily human life. Each facet and form requires its own special skillset to really bring them to life and I hope this book has shown you enough in terms of how to achieve that.

When you understand how to effectively persuade people to your mode of reasoning and manipulate them without their knowledge, you are bound to get more out of situations regardless of whether they are business or relationship scenarios. Eventually, being able to manipulate people to your advantage would increase your influence in life and this influence would bring you success.

Good luck in using the skills you have learned from this book and I hope you experience as much joy in learning as I enjoyed in making this book.

A final word of advice, never give up easily; nothing good ever comes easy and practice makes perfect.

Dark Psychology
Proven Manipulation Techniques to Influence Human Psychology

Discover Secret Methods For Mind Control, Dark NLP, Deception, Subliminal Persuasion, and Dark Hypnosis

Table of Contents

Chapter 1: Introduction to Dark Psychology 91
- Persuasion 96
- Manipulation 96
- Deception 97
- Subliminal Messages 98
- NLP – Neuro-Linguistic Programming 100

Chapter 2: Body Language and Lies 103
- Body Language 103
- Deception 107
- The Deception Spectrum 108
- Deceptive Topics 109
- Deceptive Tactics 112

Chapter 3: NLP 115
- NLP: A Brief History 120
- The Pillars Of Nlp: How To Apply The Knowledge In This Guide 121
- NLP Presuppositions 122

Chapter 4: Psychology of Influence, Persuasion And Manipulation 135

Chapter 5: Brainwash and Hypnotism 144
- Hypnotism Is Real 144
- Hypnotic Tactics 144
- Brainwashing 152

Brainwashing Contexts 153

The Process Of Brainwashing 155

The Impact Of Brainwashing 158

Conclusion **161**

Chapter 1: Introduction to Dark Psychology

It's a bit of a well-kept secret that the ability to manipulate people is a useful tool. It's one of the reasons how businessmen and politicians get and hold their positions. There comes a certain point in your life wherein completely turning off your emotions and being pragmatic is a skill you need to have. Nobody likes to discuss it because we have this societal fear of the reality that people can just be seen as a means to an end.

The late Steve Jobs was particularly renowned for his ability to work people's emotions and to say just the right thing that would get them to come around to his view. It was so strong, in fact, that the people around him developed their own term for it: the 'reality distortion field,' a phrase coined from a similar phenomenon in the Star Trek universe.

There are numerous historical instances of Steve Jobs taking advantage of his unique ability to get precisely what he wanted. One such instance was when Jobs, in the 1980s, was trying to get Pepsi CEO John Sculley to come to Apple. This exchange spawned a famous line that many know today: "Do you want to sell sugared water for the rest of your life, or do you want to come with me and change the world?"

There is a lot that can be said about his specific ability to charm and manipulate people, not the least of which was his deep understanding of what people wanted as well as what people wanted to hear. Add on to this an understanding of subtle intimidation, power cues, and a large amount of passion and charisma, and you have a powerhouse who could get pretty much whatever he wanted.

How does all of this apply to you? Well, you're reading this because you want to learn how to work with people from the inside out. You want to know how to say just the right thing to get what you need and how to manipulate people such that you can bypass any obstacles, so they will do exactly what you want. If that's the case, then you've come to the right place.

Dark Psychology

The fact is that the mind is a relatively simple thing. While the brain is infinitely complex, the manifestations of the conscious mind are both resolute and easy to work with. Most people work in very obvious and predictable ways such that if they're a 'normal' person, you can rather easily figure out the best way to work with them in no time flat.

The purpose is to analyze all of these patterns within the context of people in general so that you can learn the best way to put these trends to use. Some people will, of course, break these 'standard' molds, and for this reason there are a couple chapters dedicated to the idea of knowing the person you're working with, reading their inner and outer body language and mental cues, and knowing how to build a paradigm that you can easily manipulate them with.

In the end, this is about using the concept of neuro-linguistic programming to its fullest to get what you want out of people. A more common term for this is 'manipulation.' However, the aim of neuro-linguistic programming is slightly different. Neuro-linguistic programming is more focused on the long-term shifting of attitudes where manipulation is more based on immediate gains. That isn't to say that neuro-linguistic programming isn't a form of manipulation though, it absolutely is.

When you hear the term 'manipulation,' you will probably have some sort of knee-jerk reaction like, "Wait, isn't manipulation wrong?" And to this question, there is no simple answer.

I have to say no, though. Manipulation isn't wrong, manipulation is simply a tool. How you use it can determine whether it's wrong or not. For example, an example of manipulation being objectively wrong is doing something that gets somebody terribly hurt. There are also some unspoken rules that you should never break. For example, while it's pretty easy to take advantage of the fact that somebody's parent is dying, actually doing so is a major ethical gray area.

If you stick to maintaining an ethical approach, then manipulation actually proves itself as a method of understanding people and knowing how to work with them so things will work out better for you. You can even use manipulation for good purposes. One such example is Steve Jobs yet again, who used his reality distortion field for good causes, such as when he would convince his employees that it was possible to do something that was more or less impossible, which in turn, would make them work harder for the end result and eventually lead to a new mark being set in technology.

We all know that psychology is the study and analysis of the human mind and human behavior. So, what is Dark Psychology? It is the science and art of manipulating and controlling the human mind through various methods. Psychology is central to human interactions, thoughts, and actions whereas Dark Psychology involves the use of tactics of persuasion, motivation, coercion, and manipulation to get what you want.

There is a phenomenon in this realm referred to as the Dark Psychology Triad that consists of elements that help in detecting potential criminal behavior in people. The Dark Triad is a combination of traits including Narcissism, Machiavellianism, and Psychopathy. What are the characteristic features of each of these Dark Triad traits?

- Narcissism – is related to lack of empathy, high levels of egotism, and grandiosity

- Machiavellianism – People with this attitude have little or no sense of morality and ruthlessly employ manipulation and other tactics to exploit and/or deceive others.

- Psychopathy – These people come across as very charming and charismatic and deep down are highly impulsive, selfish, lack empathy, and are fairly remorseless.

Yes, it is true that none of us wants to be manipulated and yet it happens in our daily lives with unerring regularity, many times unwittingly. Additionally, we also use mind control and manipulation tactics to try and get what we want. Dark Psychology involves studying the psychodynamics of people who prey on and victimize others to achieve their own ends.

There are people who use dark psychology tactics knowingly and with the intention to cause harm to others and there are those who use or are prey to these tactics in unwitting ways. Moreover, it is a survival instinct in all living beings to be wary of our surroundings and use guile and deception to survive and thrive. There are multiple studies that prove this innate ability to victimize others.

Although we believe that we have control over our actions and reactions, under extreme pressure, it is very difficult to predict our behaviors and there are high chances that many employ dark tactics to escape from these pressures. The following studies are examples of how human minds behave in unpredictable ways when compelled or sometimes even when it may not have needed such an extreme reaction.

Let us look at some of these experiments conducted in the '60s and '70s by psychologists. While there are controversies surrounding the experiments and plausible rationalizations were provided in retrospect, it goes without doubt that the human mind can be very unpredictable and is capable of reaching out to its dark aspects with little or no provocation.

The 'learner' was actually only an actor.

If the learner gave a wrong answer, the volunteers were told to give electric shocks by turning the 'dial', which had labels ranging from mild pain to extreme pain to even fatal. The experimenter wearing a lab coat told the volunteers that they should continue to increase the intensity of the 'electric shock' until the right answer was given by the learner. The volunteers could hear the simulated screams of the learner from the other room. If the volunteer did not want to increase the intensity, then the experiment told them to continue employing the following statements:

- Please continue
- The experiment needs you to go on
- It is essential that you go on
- You have no choice; you have to go on

There were startling and disturbing outcomes from this rather controversial experiment. Despite hearing the simulated screams of extreme pain from the 'learners,' 65% of the volunteers turned the knob to 'fatal.' They did not even bother to ask about the health of the learner. Yet, most of the volunteers said that they would have never behaved this way but did not find the wherewithal to stand up to a figure of authority (lab-coated experimenter). Dark Psychology is easy to trigger, isn't it?

The most disturbing observation of these kinds of experiments was the fact that the volunteers were not even aware that they were being manipulated and that they were delving into the dark aspects of their minds. Another study which proved the unconscious behavior under authority goes as follows:

A group of volunteers was asked to watch a screen in which a basketball game was going on. They were told to count the number of passes that took place between players wearing white shirts. At some point during the game, a person dressed in a gorilla costume walked into the court. The participants were so engrossed in counting the number of passes that they did not even notice this aberration. In fact, many participants swore that no such disturbance took place! They were unconsciously following the orders of the experimenter.

Another common dark psychology tactic is called 'priming' in which people's behaviors can be changed without them even realizing it. For example, read this sentence, 'The house was so old that it groaned, creaked, and struggled to stand on its shaky foundation.' Now, suppose you were to stand up, chances are very high that you will unconsciously have taken care to do so at a slower pace than usual as you were just now 'primed' for old age.

Politicians are known to use priming to change voting preferences based on the location of the booth. Like this, there are many studies which prove that accessing and employing the dark side of our minds is not just easy but can happen without us even being aware of it.

Moreover, these theories have been applied and checked repeatedly throughout the history of mankind and dark psychology is an integral part of our minds. This is not the same as conspiracy theories. Dark psychology only represents the innate need and desire for man to dominate over others who are weaker than himself so as to achieve his own ends. Marketing advertisements are classic examples of manipulating the minds of the buyers and convincing them to buy the product, which they may or may not need.

Therefore, it makes sense to know, understand, and appreciate this aspect of our minds and use strategies and tips to 'prime' our minds and those of others in ways that will result in win-win situations for all concerned stakeholders.

Persuasion

Persuasion is one of the most popular forms of mind control. This method is used in so many different areas of life that many people don't even recognize when it is happening. That is exactly why it works.

Persuasion is not the same as convincing, although most people believe the two are the same thing. However, persuasion is the act of skillfully encouraging someone to do what you want them to do without them realizing you're doing it, whereas convincing someone means that you are using tactics that are easy to recognize. To explain it a bit further, persuading means to skillfully present facts and information in a way that doesn't make it obvious that you are doing so, and encouraging people to do what you desire for them to do. Convincing people, on the other hand, is very obvious and often includes a lot of back-and-forth and ultimately nagging, begging, or pleading someone to make the decision you want them to make after they have already chosen the alternative.

When you are learning about persuasion, it may seem easy. In reality, it is a strategy that requires a lot of time, effort, and practice. You cannot simply read about persuasion and then run out and master it. Instead, you really need to ensure that you grasp the concept and that you practice putting it into action in your daily life. In chapter 6 you will learn about many real-life strategies that can help you further integrate this technique into your life.

Manipulation

Manipulation tends to be regarded as one of the darker methods of mind control, and many people think it is a nasty thing to do. However, when you learn to use manipulation properly, you can use it to gain control over virtually anyone's mind and have your desired effect on their decisions and actions.

Unlike persuasion, which is typically comprised of conversational tactics, manipulation involves external influences to help encourage people to do what you want them to do. These include strategies like building trust, and proving why they should do what you want them to do. While some of these strategies are conversational, they are often impacted by external influences unlike persuasion which relies merely on wording structure and methods of structuring your sentences and conversations.

Deception

Deception is an extremely sophisticated strategy that is used in mind control. This is not the process of outright lying to people, but rather tactfully covering up certain pieces of information to avoid them from ever being discovered. This strategy allows people to knowingly omit information from conversations without being considered liars since they have never directly been asked, and therefore they have never directly lied.

When you are partaking in deception, you have to be tactful and consistent in keeping the conversation away from any question that may put you in a position where you must either come clean or actually lie. Using deception as a secondary manipulation method for mind control purposes means controlling the conversation and preventing it from ever going in the direction that would suggest information that you are lying or covering up information.

In order to skillfully use deception, you need to know how to guide the conversation in a way that leads the listener to believe something without ever actually being told to believe it. For example, if you want to prevent someone from finding out that you are attracted to someone they also like, you could create the illusion that you are not. You never actually admit that you aren't, you just lead the conversation so that it can be assumed that you aren't.

This is a powerful form of mind control because it allows you to deny ever doing anything wrong. Since you have never admitted to anything or lied about anything, you can easily say that it was the listeners fault for not asking, or for assuming anything was implied.

Subliminal Messages

When you use subliminal messages, you are sending messages without someone actually knowing that you are doing so. These messages tend to slip past the conscious mind and directly into the subconscious. The powerful thing about subliminal messages is that you can be telling someone one thing, and yet having them hear something entirely different. While this conscious mind digests something that they are willingly accepting, their subconscious mind may be hearing something entirely different. Because you have put them into a receptive mode, they are more likely to react and respond in the way that you want them to, and their subconscious mind is more likely to accept the information as well.

Subliminal messaging is powerful because it allows you to control the mind without any indication that you are doing so. You can speak directly through the conscious mind and into the subconscious mind, thus planting information, evidence, and knowledge into the subconscious that encourages your listener to support your position and act or think in the way that you want them to. You are literally programming their mind with your desired messages, and they have no idea that you are doing so.

Mind control is a very powerful strategy that can enable you to have people thinking in your favor. These individuals are going to unknowingly be listening extremely closely to your sentences and hanging on your every word, while giving into anything you want. Because of your masterful ability to control their minds without them even knowing it, you will be able to have any desired outcome effortlessly.

People often have a few different traits which you can use to understand them. Things such as their body language, their life situation, and their emotions. All of these impact one another. In the following chapters, we will break down all of these aspects to help you understand exactly what position you're in.

Body language is a huge giveaway about what's going on in a person's head. Understand that in terms of neuro-linguistic programming, body language is a language in and of itself.

Dark Psychology

We're going to expand on this concept just a bit so we can gain an understanding of how we can read and process other people's emotions.

This is actually a very critical part of neuro-linguistic programming, and one of the things that makes it such a challenge. Doing it properly is not like picking a lock. There is no 'correct' path for you to do it right. It's a very dynamic activity, which is heavily centered on your ability to understand what the other person is thinking in a very concrete manner.

Understand that a person has many physical tells, but that's not the be-all-end-all of what is going on in a person's mind. Some people are so good at hiding their emotions that you can't really tell what's going on under the hood unless you know them very well.

Often, people will have two emotions running in parallel. These can be difficult to decipher, but generally, they have the emotion at their foreground — this is what they display themselves to be feeling — and they have their emotion in the background, which is what they are feeling under the hood.

Some people are worse than others when it comes to hiding their emotions while some people make no effort at all. There are times, too, where these emotions may run in tandem and are exactly the same.

The truth is, though, that if you're trying to convince somebody of something, you always have to consider the possibility that people don't often feel what they're projecting themselves to be feeling. Usually, you have to consider what these parallel emotions could be.

We'll focus more on the underlying emotions when we get to the chapter on psychoanalysis. However, for now, we just need to focus primarily on reading emotions on the surface.

People convey a lot of their emotions through their body language as well as through their tone of voice and their choice of words.

If you pay attention to a person's eyes, you can read a lot into somebody's foreground emotion. While, hopefully, you're emotionally competent enough to read foreground emotions relatively well, note that some of these can be difficult to break apart from one another. For example, while the difference between annoyance and anger are slight in terms of their physical display, they have far different emotional connotations. Annoyance is much shorter and less severe, though perhaps more immediately snappy. Anger is more brooding and harder to work your way out of.

Their tone of voice will also tell you a lot. Often, when people aren't being completely honest about the emotion they're presenting, their voice will sound ever so slightly off. Being able to recognize this and using context clues to figure out what's really bothering them or going on in their head is very important.

Sometimes their choice of words will give you hints as well. Pay attention and try to notice if their sentences are structured differently. Are they shorter? Is their choice of words more serious than usual?

In essence, pay attention to a person's body language, as it will tell you a lot about what you need to know when it comes to what a person is feeling, at least on the surface level. When you combine that with your analysis of their underlying conditions, you actually get a very potent piece of information that you can work with.

NLP – Neuro-Linguistic Programming

NLP involves the three most powerful elements that contribute to the human experience and they are; neurology, language, and programming. So, how can we use NLP to influence people? Here are some answers to that.

NLP techniques are in use both in businesses and personal relationships to influence people around you. NLP techniques are designed to help you get your message across in the correct way so that they are interpreted by the people to give you your desired outcomes. NLP techniques also focus on the choice and appropriate use of language to help you motivate people around you to get something good done.

NLP techniques are designed in such a way that if used correctly, they can help you teach others how to become more productive and efficient in their lives which, in turn, helps you in your life as well. NLP techniques are also designed for salespeople so that they are able to reach the subconscious levels of the buyers' minds in such a way that they feel good and happy about buying the product or service.

The basic presumption of NLP is that each of us is unique in the way we think, we interpret, and the way we present ourselves to the outside world. NLP says that if we know how we think, then we can be empowered to change the way we think. Extending the same logic outside of us, if we know how people think, we can empower ourselves and them to influence changes in their thought processes.

Let us take an example. Each of us has a unique way of translating what we see around us into thoughts. Our preference could be to the use of sight, sound or touch or a unique combination of all three. If our preferred sense is that of sight, then we easily convert the events in our life into pictures and images in our thoughts. If our preferred sense is that of touch, we easily convert our experiences into feelings.

Let's take this a bit further. Suppose you had a preference for the sense of sight. This preferred sense is actually very evident in the way you interact with others. For example, you will use phrases like, 'See you later,' or 'I can see how this will turn out,' etc. You will normally be the type of person who decides that when something or someone is out of sight, then that person or thing is out of your mind too.

So, with a person whose sense preference is that of touch, phrases such as 'Catch you later,' or 'I'm getting a bad feeling from this,' etc. will be used. So, by knowing these preferences and the way they become evident through their language and thought, we can understand people better and once we understand their behavior, we can more easily influence the way they think.

It is a natural thing to be fond of those individuals who are like us in the way they think and behave. So, by knowing their preferred means of communication, we can use the same way to communicate with them and therefore make it easy for us to influence them.

A classic example of NLP influencing technique is to synchronize your breathing with that of the other person. Watch when the person breathes in and you match your inhalation with that. When you match every breath of yours with the other person's, you will find an invisible connection to the individual giving you a great boost in terms of influencing his or her thoughts.

Chapter 2: Body Language and Lies

Body Language

Humans are adept at reading body language or the nonverbal signals we use to communicate. These nonverbal cues can communicate more information that the words we choose. From facial expressions to how we stand, the things we don't say convey volumes of information.

People have a natural inclination to engage in helping behavior. Our communal nature makes it imperative to understand the meaning behind nonverbal cues. This makes every person on earth a mind reader. It just so happens that some people are better at it than others.

Our communities aren't a big homogenous mass though. We divide up into micro and macro groups and prioritize our "tribe" when making decisions. In the long run, it provides significant benefits to team up rather than every person for themselves.

But our mind-reading abilities add a layer of complexity. Humans can lie or otherwise hide their true intentions. This often provides a significant short-term advantage at the cost of ill will from others in the community.

Deception is an active performance. It requires decent brain power and effort to maintain a ruse for any length of time. We can only focus on a few things at a time so our body language often gives away our true thoughts and intentions.

I have learned a few tricks that can help anyone improve their ability to influence others through body language. They are simple but have helped everyone from vacuum salesmen to Ted Bundy hide their true intentions.

These techniques aren't going to stop racism, misogyny or ass-hats. But they can pressure others to respond in subtle or overt ways. With enough practice and proper execution, they will push people over the fence of suspicion and help you change a no into a yes.

Practice Perfect Posture: When I walk into a room, people immediately know that I am the one in charge. I don't have to tell them I'm in charge, they have already decided I am before I even open my mouth. I communicate this information to them primarily through posture.

Posture communicates our status within a group more than the clothes on our back and the words coming from our mouths. It only takes a second for someone to start making decisions about me. So I make sure to instantly communicate authority and power through the way I hold my body.

I stand and gesture using specific techniques that subtly show dominance and control without seeming like a tyrant or manipulative. These techniques include standing erect, using gestures with palms facing down, and with filling my space.

The brain is programmed to equate power with the amount of space they take up. Standing straight makes you look taller and holding the shoulders back maximizes the space I take up. But if I slouched, I appear project submission and weakness.

Maintaining good posture helps others understand that I am someone worth knowing. While using my space to make broad and expansive gestures shows others I know my limits. These combine to command respect and help others to value engaging with me.

Adopt a Likable Tone: Coming into an interaction defensively or acting like I want to fight is naturally off-putting. It sets me up to be rejected and makes the other person retract. If my intention is to influence a subject, I need them open and welcoming, not closed and defensive.

So I approach them as an old friend, helping them relax slightly and naturally open up. By showing I am comfortable, it signals to others that they should be as well. It's surprising how welcoming people can be when they relax a bit.

By acting friendly and open, they almost instinctively respond with warmth. They may remain suspicious of your intentions if you overplay it though. So be friendly, not fake, and believe that people want to help.

Example: When I meet someone for the first time, I smile and introduce myself in a familiar way and ask something about them. I begin my encounter on the basis that we are old friends meeting again. This helps me with the next trick...

Mirror Body Language: One of the most important elements of attraction is believing that the other person understands you on a deep level. The feeling of someone just getting you is intoxicating. The more we feel they understand us the deeper our connection.

It's important to emphasize commonalities rather than differences. The more we have in common, the more likely we are to align our motives and goals. These situations show us that the other person is similar to us. Since body language communicates the most information in the shortest time, it's the best way to establish that feeling of similarity.

People naturally mirror body language. We often don't think about our stance, tone, and position in conversation consciously. By monitoring and mirroring the other person's body language, it sets them up to be more attracted to me and value my opinion higher.

Example: Be subtle! If the other person shifts their weight to lean against a wall, lean up against it too. If they talk with their hands, I make sure to gesture when I talk. If they cross their legs, I do the same but in a slightly different position. I don't make huge changes, just enough to be in sync with the other person.

Establish Control: Once we are in sync, I begin to lead the conversation. I continually build rapport and when the time is right I begin changing my body language to encourage them to mirror me. Once they follow my lead, I know that I am in control and can diffuse an intense situation or build excitement.

The fastest way to gain trust is to mirror the other person's body language. Before I start leading, I have to get them to be in sync with me. The better I can do at mirroring and tone, the faster they sync up and I gain control of the conversation.

Questions help establish control of a conversation. It may seem counter-intuitive, but the person giving answers is weaker than the person asking the questions. So I ask questions as often as possible, although I rarely give the other person time to answer them.

Once in control, I can lead the conversation where I want. All the while I watch and study their reactions. I keep tailoring my questions and responses to encourage the other person to respond emotionally. The more emotion I can work up, the more control I have.

Example: If I want to convince a person to sign a contract, I control the conversation by asking questions and mirroring their body language. I'll cross my legs if they cross theirs and make similar gestures as my subject. Once their body language starts syncing up with mine, I ask questions like, "What are you going to do once you sign?" and "I can't believe we managed to get these terms. You must feel pretty lucky right?"

Make Eye Contact: We are the only primates in the world with white in our eyes. That's because we use them as a primary way to communicate. The eye is called the window to the soul because of how integral it is to body language.

Without good eye contact, people will perceive you as nervous, shifty, or unattractive. Making eye contact with someone creates an intense connection. That connection is integral to appearing trustworthy and engaged.

This doesn't mean to stare people down. Eyes can communicate aggression as easily as timidity. Refusing to break eye contact can make others uncomfortable and appear overly intense.

Example: I maintain eye contact for about 80% of my interactions. When the other person is talking, I maintain eye contact unless they are talking about something in eyesight or are becoming overly excited. I lower my eyes to communicate sadness, raise them for praise and keep my eyes mainly on the speaker.

Give Good Face: When talking about body language, we tend to focus on the torso and limbs. Things like posture, where and when to touch someone and how to hold our hands dominate the conversation. We often underestimate the power of emotive expressions.

It always surprises me how effective a smile is in communicating emotions. It can indicate pleasure, happiness, irony, appeasement, or a superiority complex. A genuine smile is one of the most underrated aspects of attraction.

We are the only primates that smile at people we like. The others see it as a threat display. People naturally find a mouth full of pearly white teeth to be very attractive.

Just make sure any smile you give is genuine. When people realize you are faking a smile, it sours their disposition. It gives away that you are deceiving them and calls everything you do and say into question.

Deception

Deception is a key aspect of dark psychology. Like many other dark psychological tactics, it can be difficult to tell whether any given instance of deception is dark or not. Before we explore the difference between dark and normal deception, let's first understand exactly what deception is.

A lot of people would state the viewpoint that lying and deception are the same thing. This is inaccurate. Lying is a form of deception but is by no means the only form deception can take. Rather than thinking of deception as "lies" it is better to think of it as "misleading." Any action or word capable of making someone believe something other than the truth can be accurately termed deception.

So what are some common manifestations of deception? Lying, omitting the truth, implying falsehood or fraudulently providing evidence for something false are all examples of deception. You will probably realize that you have done some of these things at some point yourself. Does that mean that all acts of deception are examples of dark psychology? Not at all.

Everyone deceives to some extent or another. People might deceive others for a range of reasons such as kindness, embarrassment or feelings of inadequacy. For example, studies have shown that many, even most men will lie about their height on dating websites. This does not make them practitioners of dark psychology! People even deceive themselves about a range of issues including their health, ambition, and happiness. Such regular, day-to-day examples of deception do not equate to dark deception. So what does?

Deception can be seen as dark when it is carried out with either a negative or indifferent intention toward the person being deceived. Normal deception is usually motivated by an inability to face up to the truth in one way or another. Dark deception, on the other hand, is an understanding that the truth does not serve the deceptive aims of the deceiver. Therefore, the truth is either changed, hidden, or ignored in favor of a version of events that better suits the purpose of the person deceiving.

Put simply, people who deploy dark psychology use deception to harm, not help. They help their own interests, but at any cost, regardless of who gets hurt.

Some people assume that if a deception is small scale it cannot be seen as dark, whereas larger deceptions must be inherently dark. This is not the case. By exploring the idea of the deception spectrum you will see that it is not the size of a deception that determines whether it is dark or not, rather the purpose behind the deception.

The Deception Spectrum

To understand the idea of deception it is important to understand that it can occur on either a large or a small scale. One of the main mistakes that people often make is assuming that deception is only serious if it is big and does not matter if it is small. This is a grave error. Small deceptions can be used in a powerfully dark way by skilled manipulators and are often more effective than large deceptions. Similarly, some of the largest deceptions ever carried out have been performed by deliberate manipulators to serve their own aims and objectives. Dark examples of various types of deception, large and small, will now be presented to illustrate the idea of the deception spectrum.

So what are some of the ways that smaller deceptions can be used by people who practice the art of dark psychology? Often, small deceptions are used initially to test the victim's gullibility and condition them into believing the deceptive statements and actions of the manipulator. If people are conditioned to believe a range of smaller lies over time, they are more likely to believe a larger lie in the future. This gradual conditioning is not the only way smaller deceptions can be used as a dark psychological weapon.

Smaller deceptions can also be carried out to undermine a victim's trust in their own powers of logic and reason. If a manipulator deceives a victim over small issues, and the victim begins to question what is happening, the victim may well conclude that their suspicion is irrational and they therefore cannot trust their own judgment. Most people are more likely to conclude that their own judgment is faulty, rather than another person is deceiving them over seemingly small issues. Users of dark psychology are aware of this general "trust" that people have and seek to exploit it without mercy.

Large-scale deception can also be an example of dark psychology in practice. One of the largest deceptions possible is to convince someone that you are a different person than you say you are. Not in terms of personality or some other detail. An entire identity. Name, date of birth, everything! The most skilled users of dark psychology are able to persuade other people to buy in entirely into their portrayal of a false identity and background.

Now that it has been shown how manipulative users of dark psychology are able to use the deception spectrum for their own aims, we will explore some of the most common topics and subjects that people are deceived about. We will then look at exactly how these large- and small-scale deceptions are carried out by exploring the specific tactics that are used.

Deceptive Topics

Everyone has heard the old saying that "money is the root of all evil." This is an exaggeration, but money is certainly the route of many deceptions. Deception and money can cross paths in many different ways. Some people deceive to attain money, others deceive to hide their own money, or lack thereof. Because money is such a common topic, some of its deceptive uses will now be explored.

Dark Psychology

One of the most common dark psychology deceptions involving money is carried out by the professional beggar. These are individuals that aim to extract money from the public despite having plenty of it. These beggars draw on a number of dark psychological principles to get money from innocent victims. Such beggars have been known to inflict injuries upon their own body to appear more desperate to victims. Some of the most extreme deceivers in this area have even turned their own children into heroin addicts to use them as part of their scam. This is an example of the depths that money-related deception can sink to.

Marital status is another common area where people choose to deceive. Sometimes, people try and hide their married background to seduce a new victim. This can be for either financial or sexual or other reasons. Some people have multiple wives spread out across the world who do not know about each other. This type of deception has become harder with the advent of the Internet and the ability to check up on people via social media. The best deceivers are able to hide their tracks expertly and keep each fraudulent wife separate from the next.

Some people choose to appear falsely married when they are in fact not! This type of deception can occur for several reasons. A married couple is often perceived as more trustworthy than a couple that is not married. Some users of dark psychology are aware of this perception and use it for their own schemes and plans. Some people pretend to be married for reasons related to tax and insurance. One of the most common deceptions of this type is the creation of a fictional dead husband or wife to gain people's sympathy and, often, their money as a result.

A criminal background is another area of life many people are deceptive about. This is because it is almost impossible to be trusted professionally or personally if you have committed certain crimes. For example, if a man meets a woman, and the man has committed a serious crime in his past, how likely is he to tell the woman he has just met about this? It seems doubtful that he would be entirely upfront. Interestingly, such deception is not always dark. If the man does it through fear of being rejected, this is not dark deception. If he does it with the intention of hiding the truth to later harm his new victim, then this is a clear indication of dark psychology at work.

Dark Psychology

One of the most evil and deplorable examples of deception related to criminality is when someone who has committed serious past offences, such as rape, hides these in order to commit similar actions in the future. People with a dark psyche of this type are often compelled by their abnormal urges to the point they will do literally anything to hide the truth and carry on giving in to their compulsions.

Manipulators also feel that deception is a great way to hide any abnormal or socially unacceptable feelings they have. This stops their victim from being alerted to the kind of person they really are until it is too late. For example, if someone who uses dark psychology is interested in a person only for sex, they know this focus is likely to be a red flag to their victim and will therefore deceive their victim. They may either overtly lie or imply that their true intention is love and commitment. The victim falls for the deception, the manipulator's exploitation is complete and yet another person is hurt by deception.

One of the most common areas to be deceptive in is the truth of a manipulator's personal feelings for a victim. Deception is the most powerful tool the manipulator has to influence a victim to perceive things in the way the manipulator wishes, rather than how they really are. Typically, deception will be used in relation to interpersonal feelings to portray the manipulator as something they are not. Some of the most common examples of this use of deception will now be provided.

Within the field of romantic relationships, deception is often used to mask the manipulator's true intentions. Deceptive words and actions will leave a victim feeling as if the manipulator "just happens to be" what they are looking for at that particular time in their life. In actual fact, skilled manipulators are able to identify vulnerable people and probe their psychological needs and weak points. This information can then be used to deceptively cloak the manipulator and make them appear to be something they are not, but something the victim wishes they were. This deception is often the starting point of more complex, long-term manipulations.

Deception can also be used to soften up the victims' feelings in a non-romantic context and increase their susceptibility to manipulation. If, for example, a manipulator is looking for a vulnerable person to use dark psychology against, they may initially portray their own intentions as innocent. Even if the intention is to become intensely close to a person, the manipulator will usually deceptively portray himself as a very casual, easy-going person. This deception can be prolonged if needed. The manipulator will be whatever the victim needs, for as long as the victim needs, in order to get their guard down and allow the thorough manipulation to begin.

Deceptive Tactics

You now understand what exactly dark deception is, its spectrum and the common areas people are deceived about. Now it is time to examine closely the specific tactics used by manipulators to darkly deceive. Each of the tactics is equally powerful and careful manipulators know exactly how to use each at its most impactful and harmful time. It is important to note that manipulators will not neatly alternate between the four following categories—any given deception is likely to involve a blend of each.

Lying is perhaps the most obvious and common form of dark deception. It is likely to be chosen as a technique when the manipulator has decided that their victim is susceptible to lies and unable to gauge the truth. This may be because the victim is a generally trusting person or that the manipulator has carefully worked on their target over time to lower their guard. If a manipulator has chosen to deceive through the use of lies then it is likely they have also thought of a way to hide their lies and explain any discrepancies the victim may notice. Manipulators are masters of having a "plan b" at any given time during their dark deception.

Deception through lying is likely to occur in a subtle and thought out way. A skilled deceiver is likely to embed their lie into truthful information over time. For example, a manipulator will probably tell a story that is 90% true and 10% false. The victim will perceive the story as entirely true and not have any way of separating and ascertaining the truth regarding the deceptive 10%. Some manipulators also spend time associating truth with a particular tone of voice or gesture. They can then say something falsely deceptive in this tone of voice, or with this gesture, and it is likely to be perceived as true by their victim's subconscious.

Implying is a more subtle form of deception than out and out lying. Implying involves suggesting something false is true rather than boldly stating it is. Let's illustrate this idea with an example. If someone wanted to deceive a victim about the amount of money they have then they could either lie or imply. A lie would sound something like "Oh I'm a successful guy. I've made a lot of money," while the manipulator is well aware this is not the case. An implication may take the form of "it's so stressful trying to handle things with my accountant. Trying to get my tax bill down takes a lot of my time." The manipulator has acted and spoken in a way that implies they are wealthy without flatly stating it.

Manipulators often favor implications, such as those just mentioned, as they provide plausible deniability. If the victim accuses the manipulator of lying, the manipulator can say they did no such thing, and technically be truthful. Implications are also powerful if a victim happens to have an active imagination. The deceptive implication can be seen as a seed planted in the mind of the victim. The victim's own imagination then does the manipulator's work for them and fills in the blank spaces to create an idealized version of reality, according to the manipulator's prompts.

Omission is a failure to mention something that is true. This stands in contrast with other forms of deception such as lies or implications. Both lies and implications use falsehood to cover truth, to varying degrees. Omission instead goes the route of simply ignoring the truth and leading the victim's attention away from it. For example, if a manipulative user of dark psychology had an aspect of their past they did not want their victim to focus on, they would simply never mention it. They would draw attention to other times in their past or swerve the subject whenever possible.

One way omission is often carried out is by creating an "emotional fence" around a situation. This is a tactic in which a manipulator implies that a particular period of their life, or topic, is too painful or uncomfortable to discuss. The victim will then avoid talking about this time, or asking awkward questions, of their own volition. If the victim does bring up the subject the manipulator wishes to avoid then the manipulator can play the "it's too painful" card. This allows them to avoid the truth while making the victim feel guilty for touching on a "painful topic"!

Fraud is the most elaborate and criminal form of deception used by those who deploy dark psychology. Think of fraud as a lie on steroids. Instead of simply lying about something from their past, a fraudulent dark deceiver will have false documents, stories, and other evidence to back up their lie. The most skillful deceivers will use such things in a subtle way. Rather than saying, "no, I really am a Doctor, look at my certificate!" they are likely to make subtle displays such as leaving the fraudulent evidence around for their victims to see for themselves. Deceivers know that if they are too "pushy" with their fraudulent claims then the victim will intuit that something is wrong.

Worryingly, fraud is more common than ever thanks to the prevalence of computers and the Internet. Deceivers are able to use professional-grade software to quickly and easily make realistic-looking documents of almost any type. Such frauds can be carried out for either personal or professional reasons. Some of the most serious types of professional fraud include instances where people have obtained jobs using a false identity, stolen from a company, and then disappeared before their identity can ever be known. Personal frauds include terrifying tales such as people with HIV spreading the disease with the help of falsely produced certificates of clean sexual health.

When dark deception enters the realm of fraudulence it is a sign that the deceiver is a dangerous and committed user of dark psychology. For a person to risk running afoul of the law and facing serious criminal charges, they have to be truly committed to the manipulation they are attempting. If many users of dark deception are amateurs, the deceptive fraudsters are the dangerous professionals that must be avoided at all costs.

Ironically, one of the main ways dark deception is often carried out effectively is following the manipulator's own pantomime of feeling deceived by their victim! Many manipulators know that, by portraying their victim as the deceptive party, they are able to deflect any attention away from their own deceptive efforts. This is an example of a deception within a deception and shows the complex, layered approach to manipulation that many deceivers use.

Chapter 3: NLP

Neuro-linguistic programming (NLP) is an approach to communication, personal development, and psychotherapy created by Richard Bandler and John Grinder in California in the 1970s that leverages the power of language to influence thought.

NLP has infiltrated every element of modern business life. Everyone in sales or marketing has practiced these methods to some degree, but psychoanalysts and occult leaders around the world give it a bad name.

Most people don't grasp the underlying principles and struggle to apply them in everyday environments.

But some skilled individuals can harness this power to give them an unbeatable advantage. The techniques are best used in a one-on-one or small group environment. The fewer people involved, the easier it is to read and apply NLP methods.

NLP is a complex subject and is often taught over the course of years. That's because it takes practice to learn the range of reactions people can express. But the promise of learning people's inner secrets makes this technique especially attractive to con artists and law enforcement.

NLP is basically a method of reading a person to understand their personality and individual quirks. NLP users watch for subtle cues that are invisible to most people and use them to control a conversation and the emotions of the people in it. Eye movement, skin flush, pupil dilation, and nervous tics all provide information.

After an initial round of observation, skilled users can mimic their subject in subtle but impactful ways. The NLP user thus opens their target to suggestion and steers them toward an intended destination.

A skilled NLP user can determine:

Which side of the brain their subject uses

Dark Psychology

People fall along a spectrum between creative and analytical. New science shows that brain function is actually distributed across the brain. But it is still helpful to think of people through this lens.

Word choice, sentence structure, and associations all reveal details about the person that uses them. I begin by looking at what my target is saying and how they present their points, then I adjust my words to be more analytical or emotional based on my subject.

Left-brained people often use words that elicit emotion or experiences. Right-brained people like to include things outside their experience or expertise.

Example: Left-brained people: "That looks fun. I bet we can squeeze in!" Right-brained people: "Is that safe? Is it rated for someone my size?"

Which sense is most important to them

We have more than the five senses (sight, sound, taste, touch, and smell) most people know about. We also have a sense of order, balance, morality and a host of others, and each of us has one or two that are more important than the rest.

I listen to see which sense is most important to my target. Then I use some of the same words they did in my reply.

Example: If vision is important to my subject, I say things like, "Do you see what I'm saying?" Audio-focused people respond better to "Can you hear where I'm coming from?" Meanwhile, I might ask a taste-oriented individual to "savor that for a moment."

How their brain stores information.

Our brains are the most complex computers we have ever come across. They store and process billions of bits of information a second. Each one functions a little differently. One of the biggest areas of divergence is in how people store information.

Some individuals have a memory like a sponge, soaking up everything near them. Others are more like a strainer that catches big chunks and allows everything to pass through. NLP techniques help people discern the difference and to what degree.

Over time, NLP users get better at keeping track of information. With enough time, users can improve their information tracking abilities to near-genius levels. This gives us an advantage over anyone who isn't as experienced or naturally gifted.

I use this information to determine how much info I need to overwhelm my subject. If I want to lose them in the details, I simply include more than they can keep straight. If I want them to follow along, I keep the details and figures to a minimum.

Example: I will occasionally remember something wrong on purpose. It's best with something small like a phone number or address. If my subject corrects me, I can see how well they store information. The average person can only hold seven numbers in their head at once so it normally only takes me asking for them to remember two phone numbers to see where they fall along the spectrum.

When they are lying or making things up.

People perform specific behaviors when they make things up called "tells." NLP users like me can pick up on these tells and be able to call out the liar as they lie. Some people are better than others at lying but everyone has at least one tell.

Skilled liars understand that for someone else to believe their lie, so must they. So they convince themselves of it first. They often don't display all the signs of dishonesty because they truly believe the lie as they tell it.

Practice can help people fall for their own lie but the process demands a selective memory. This feature is more reliably detected than the oft-cited slight downward glance. It also proves to be a more consistent indicator of ingrained deception than awkward looks. Power imbalances also make a refusal to make eye contact less reliable as well.

Example: When my best friend (let's call him Ted) won't look me in the eye during his story. He keeps looking down and to one side of me, then the other.

Another person (let's call him Fred) tells his story without looking away at all.

When Ted looks away I become suspicious, but Fred's refusal to look away is also a red flag. If they are subjects, I cut them some slack. As long as they don't change demeanor mid-story I can attribute some of it to simple nervousness.

How to make someone drop their guard.

NLP users like myself leverage these techniques to convince others that I am just like them. People can't help but like someone they recognize as a kindred spirit. So I combine the techniques above to highlight our similarities.

The more alike we are, the more a subject likes me. So I listen intently to what they are saying. Then I respond to them with the signals that I know appeal to their inner selves. This encourages my subjects to reveal more about themselves to me willingly.

When someone likes you, they want to include you in their lives. Listening to what they say often provides deep insight into what controls their lives. People offer up their darkest secrets willingly, believing that I truly understand them.

So you can condition people without their consent/knowledge.

Let's face it, people don't like finding out someone was manipulating them. It violates the idea that we are in control of our lives. But sometimes the truth is hard to take, and we need someone to help us see the way without calling us out on it.

We all manipulate those around us to one degree or another. This can be as simple as breaking a bad habit or establishing new relationship rules with a toxic family member. By steering them in the right direction, we can help them respond how we prefer.

NLP doesn't brainwash someone (that's covered elsewhere) or cause them to do something out of character. But it does reveal the strings that control each of us. What you do with those strings once you have them is up to you.

Once the subjects are open and receptive, I present my request in terms that they would prefer. I use strong action words with leaders, comforting and kind words with emotionally sensitive subjects, and common words with the less educated. I do everything in my power to appear similar to my subject in thought and deed. This ensures they are the most receptive to my desires and avoids having to issue orders and ultimatums.

Example: When I need a favor, I never ask for it right out the gate. Instead, I begin by building rapport. I ensure my body language is open and tailor my questions and responses to the person I am trying to influence.

Proponents of NLP believe that how you behave has a certain structure to it. Therefore, NLP aims to examine this structure to redefine the way your brain performs and responds to the information it receives. NLP helps you understand the things that make you tick. It opens your eyes to how you perceive the things that happen to you and around you on a daily basis. When you fully understand these things, you can handle situations in a better manner, and communicate more effectively.

Your neurological system is responsible for transmitting all the information your brain receives from your environment. In this context, your environment refers to everything external including all your organs- your ears, your eyes, your skin, stomach, lungs, and every other part of your body.

Your brain processes the information from all these parts of your body and transmits them to your brain and vice versa. For instance, once your brain receives information, it processes it and decides if it is good or bad news, and then transmits it to emotions that could be joy, tears, or laughter.

The takeaway here is that your brain determines how you respond to everything going on around you and how you communicate with others. Now, imagine being able to somehow, alter the way your brain handles this information and force it to react in a certain way. That is the whole logic behind NLP.

NLP helps to change your personal programming (think of computer programming: how programmers can change computer code to get a device or software to perform specific task or behave in a specific manner). It helps you re-organize your internal programming so you achieve the desired results you want.

To frame it in a simpler manner, NLP helps you achieve the following:

1. Increases Your Chances of Success: Generally, life is problematic and your day-to-day life whether at work, with your family or at leisure will be full of challenges. NLP helps you change how you view these challenges as well as your outlook on life. It helps you change the way you see life so that unimportant things stop weighing heavily on, or bothering you. It gives your life a deeper meaning and helps you organize your priorities.

It helps you identify your strengths and weaknesses so you can concentrate on things that can help you become better and more efficient, which helps you become more successful.

2. NLP Improves Your Communication Skills: NLP fosters positive thinking, which makes all your communications positive. It helps you redefine how you think and feel, which makes you a better verbal and non-verbal communicator, which then makes it easier to share your perspective with others and become.

So in essence, NLP helps you to become better at expressing yourself.

3. NLP Synchronizes Your Body and Feelings: When your mind and body are not in harmony, putting your thoughts and plans into action becomes very difficult. However, once you start using NLP, you unify your mind, body, and feelings so you can create a better connection and work towards achieving your goals.

You now have a better understanding of what NLP is and what it can do for you. Before we start using it to reprogram our behavior and maximize our potential, let us delve a bit deeper into its history:

NLP: A Brief History

John Grinder and Richard Bandler founded NLP in the 197o's at the University of Santa Cruz, California. At that time, Richard Bandler was a (AMIS) Information Sciences & Mathematics Master's level student while Dr. John Grinder was a professor of Linguistics.

They both studied people who they believed to be exceptional communicators and very good at helping their clients achieve desired results and necessary change. Particularly, they were interested in finding how it was possible for some people to effectively deal with difficult or sick people, defying the odds where other people have failed.

Grinder and Bandler chose to study three renowned psychotherapists- Virginia Satir, the developer of Conjoint Family Therapy, Fritz Perls, the founder of Gestalt psychology, and Milton Erickson, one of the major contributors to the development of Clinical Hypnotherapy. They also studied the skills of two linguists- Noam Chomsky and Alfred Korzybski, as well as social anthropologists Gregory Bateson and Psychotherapist Paul Watzlawick.

Neuro-Linguistic programming eventually exploded to include other disciplines and spread to several other countries. Unfortunately, in the 1980's, due to some dissatisfaction that Grinder had about some coding work they did together known as the 'classic code,' Blander and Grinder had a falling out. This led to a separation that led Grinder to team up with Judith Delozier to form newer models later named 'The New Code.'

Neuro-Linguistic Programming has come a very long way and many scholars have developed new codes, techniques, and versions, thus making it easier for ordinary folks to apply it in their lives to effect real transformation.

Although originally developed for use in the field of psychotherapy, professionals now apply NLP in all fields including Doctors, Accountants, Engineers, and every other profession in the world; from the way it looks, the future of NLP continues to look bright.

The Pillars Of Nlp: How To Apply The Knowledge In This Guide

To understand how to apply NLP to your personal life, you have to understand the four pillars of NLP. The four pillars of NLP are rapport, sensory awareness, outcome thinking, and behavioral flexibility.

1. Rapport: Rapport refers to how you build and maintain relationships with yourself and other people. Rapport teaches you how to say no to requests and

things you do not want while still maintaining a good professional relationship and friendships with the people whose requests you reject.

2. Sensory Awareness: Another pillar of NLP is sensory awareness; sensory awareness teaches you how to pay closer attention to the things going on around you- how to make better use of the senses of sight, sound, touch, hearing, smelling, and taste.

3. Outcome Thinking: When you face a challenge, instead of being stuck, NLP teaches you to focus on what you want and helps you make decisions that will help you achieve these things.

4. Behavioral Flexibility: This refers to how you do things and handle situations. NLP helps you to do things differently. It gives you flexibility and the ability to change a course of action when one course of action leads to failure.

Authors Romilla Ready and Kate Burton describe how the four pillars can translate into your day-to-day life with this interesting illustration.

Imagine you ordered a new software to help you record all the names, addresses, phone numbers, and other important friends and clients' details. After spending time to purchase and install the software, you discover the software does not work because it has a coding bug.

You contact the software company's customer service department and they are rude and unhelpful. At this point, you have to employ your rapport building skills with the customer service manager so they can listen to your complaints. You would need to increase your sensory awareness by listening carefully, controlling your feelings, and deciding on the most suitable response. You have to know the outcome you desire by engaging in discussions with the customer service manager; do you want a refund or a replacement. Lastly, your behavior needs to be flexible enough to accept other outcomes if the desired one is unachievable.

That is how NLP helps you to become a better communicator and helps you achieve the things that you want without a lot of stress or frustration.

NLP Presuppositions

NLP presuppositions are basic generalizations or general beliefs in NLP that can be useful to you when you act as if they are true.

Some common presuppositions of NLP include:

1. The Map is not the Territory: Alfred Korzybski takes credit for this statement. He explains that we experience the world through the human senses of sight, touch, hearing, taste, and smell, which he refers to as 'the territory.' The experiences you get from these senses then transfer to the brain where they make an internal representation that he refers to as 'the map'.

You create an internal map in your brain; your experiences shape this map, but another person who has had the same experiences would never have the same exact internal map like yours (their perceptions and the way their senses perceive information may be different). This simply means that what is outside can never be the same as what is inside your brain.

If you are a doctor, what pills mean to you may be vastly different from what they mean to a patient and even a law enforcement agent. The point is that we all make different internal representations of the same things depending on our backgrounds and personal contexts.

To be a better communicator and a generally better person, you need to learn how to see things from other people's eyes- try to understand the internal representations or map of the person you are trying to communicate with. Rather than respond negatively to other people's behavior you may deem inappropriate, focus on trying to understand why that person might have behaved that way. This would make you a happier person who accepts people's actions and inactions with greater ease.

2. There is no failure, only feedback: This very important NLP presupposition will help you, but only if you can live by it. There is no one person in the world who does not experience setbacks and failures. It is up to you to choose whether to allow those setbacks to bring you down or you want to take lessons from your setbacks and these lessons as a learning experience that helps you become better at whatever you failed at the first time when you decide to try again.

Whenever you fail at anything, rather than give up, always ask yourself these five questions:

* "What am I trying to achieve?"

* "What have I been able to achieve so far?"

* "What are the things I have learned (feedback)?"

* "How can I use the lessons learned to better my performance?"

* "How am I going to measure my performance and success?"

3. The Meaning of the Communication is the Response it elicits: How the person you are communicating with perceives the information you are trying to pass across is the most important thing. No matter how good your intentions are, your listener interprets information based on how they receive it.

The onus therefore, rests upon you to pass your messages across carefully in the way you want your listener to receive it. Before you start communicating, have a clear understanding of the desired outcome of the conversation, and then carefully construct your conversation to elicit the exact response you want.

4: If What You Are Doing Is Not Working, Do Something Different: This is yet another presupposition and a very simple one at that. Do not be fixated on things that do not work for you, instead, change your tactics.

Determine why what you are doing is not working and what you can do to get better results.

5: You have all the Resources You Need to Create Desired Outcomes: Everyone has what it takes to develop, grow, and become a better version of themselves.

6: People are Much More Than Their Behavior: The fact that a person is behaving badly does not necessarily mean he or she is bad. People behave badly when they do not have the inner resources to behave differently. Most times, helping them change or improve on these resources would help them improve their behavior and start behaving better.

7: Body Language is Important: When communicating, you have to employ the right body language because body language makes up for 55% of how others receive your communication.

For the techniques to work for you, you have to practice them. Most of the techniques listed here are not instant solutions that are going to work in one day; however, with consistent practice, your life would improve and you would get better at what you want to improve.

1st NLP Technique: Setting Personal Anchors

Anchoring focuses on helping you change your state of mind. It can help you stay calm in the face of danger or trouble, and can help you relax and behave in a positive way when people are trying to provoke you.

Anchoring tries to mimic one of Pavlov's experiments. Pavlov experimented with dogs and sounded a bell as the dogs were feeding. Whenever the dogs saw the food and heard the bells, they salivated in anticipation of the meal. After some time, Pavlov began to sound the bell without the food in sight and he noticed that the dogs salivated whenever they heard the bells even without seeing the food.

Anchors are similar; they stimulate a response in your mind and help you control your thoughts and emotions. For instance, rubbing your forehead can be an anchor. Sometimes, anchors can be involuntary. For instance, a familiar smell might bring back a memory from your childhood or a song can trigger a memory of your ex. These are examples of involuntary anchors that work automatically without any self-induced trigger.

Establishing anchors involves producing stimuli when you experience the resourceful state so that the resourceful state pairs with the anchor. Just like with the dogs that begin salivating without a meal in sight simply because they heard a bell, you can establish personal anchors that will trigger a desired response in you whenever you experience anything.

Activating the anchor refers to the act of producing the anchor after you have established it in a bid to trigger the occurrence of the resourceful state.

When you are happy or sad, you are responding to some anchors in your life. When you are feeling motivated and confident or otherwise, you are also responding to some anchors although sometimes, you do not even know what these anchors are. That is why sometimes, you may be in a bad mood without knowing why.

The NLP anchoring technique teaches you how to design personal anchors and use them to produce a desired state of mind. For instance, if you are in an interview situation and you are feeling jittery, but you want to be calm, you can use established anchors to trigger a calm response within yourself. If someone is annoying you, but you do not want to lose your temper, you can use anchors to calm yourself down.

The Resource State

In the last section, we established that we all have the resources we need to achieve the things we desire. Here, the resource state refers to memories of the required state. For instance, if you want to be calm, your resource state here is a memory of a past time where you were calm and relaxed.

The resource state involves striving to make a previous experience vivid so it feels as if you are experiencing it afresh in the present. If you cannot recall a situation where you have felt that way, you can simply just imagine yourself in the resource state.

Types of NLP Anchors

There are three different types of anchors:

1. Visual Anchors: Visual anchors involve using the things you see to provoke a response. For instance, if you want to feel powerful, you can use your wristwatch as an anchor so that any time you want to feel powerful, you simply look at the wristwatch and use it as an anchor; however, the anchor does not have to be objects- you could use people, symbols, drawings, or anything physical as an anchor.

2. Auditory Anchors: Auditory anchors involve using sounds or music as anchors to provoke a response.

3. Kinesthetic Anchors: Touching yourself or imagining someone touching you is an example of a kinesthetic anchor.

How to Set Personal Anchors

To set anchors:

1. Decide the state you wish to anchor (the response you want to elicit e.g. Calmness, happiness, feeling powerful, feeling relaxed, etc.). It is helpful to write down your intention in your journal, so that you can crystalize exactly the feeling or emotion you wish to create a trigger for.

2. Choose the anchor you want to use to trigger that state. You can use a combination of anchors such as visual and auditory anchors.

3. Close your eyes.

4. Tap into your resource state by recalling a memory where you previously experienced the state you want to trigger.

5. As soon as you can vividly recall that experience, activate the anchor (play the music, touch the parts of your body you want to use as anchors, or look at the object you wish to use).

6. Release the anchors as soon as the experience starts to fade away. It is important to release the anchor immediately the experience begins to fade so that you do not anchor a drop in that state rather than the state in itself.

7. Take a break and do something else such as counting from one to ten.

8. Repeat the process from step 1; this time, make the memory more vivid and then try to establish the anchor at the highest point of the experience.

9. Test the anchor to see if the required state occurs. After you have solidified your process, be sure to record everything about your process, to make sure that it is repeatable. What emotions came up during this process? What memories did you specifically trigger? Did you use visual or auditory cues? Write down everything.

10. Check the anchor the next day and continuously until it becomes permanent.

You should always ensure the anchor fires in the same way every time you want to link to the resourceful experience. If you cannot get a desired state when you trigger the anchor, change the anchor to avoid establishing a negative anchor.

2nd NLP Technique: Pattern Interruption

Imagine a situation where you have a favorite route you drive through each time you are going from home to your place of work (every day). This driving pattern becomes repetitive and sometimes, you do not have to place too much effort and concentration into it because well, you already know the drill.

It is kind of like autopilot for you and you take out this time to think of the tasks you need to complete at home, how your day went, and other things while your subconscious takes care of everything else.

Suddenly, you hear a loud sound and bam! A large tree has just fallen and your path is obstructed. You slam the brakes and the car comes to a screeching halt. For the next few seconds, you are sitting in your car wondering what just happened.

Your subconscious is not used to this situation; therefore, it does not know how to respond. At this point, you have to step in; your conscious mind has to take control and issues instructions detailing how to handle the situation. Your subconscious mind is great at running automatic patterns so that your conscious mind can handle other activities that need conscious handling.

When you are trying to alter some patterns, sometimes, automatic habits, thoughts, emotions, and actions can create a problem. It is not as if you are not willing to change, but your subconscious keeps pulling you back, which then cause you to do the same thing repeatedly.

Well, you have to understand that the subconscious mind is very poor at decision-making. Only the conscious mind has the ability to make decisions. As an NLP technique, pattern interruption forces your subconscious mind into a state where it waits for information from your conscious mind.

It helps you break habits and embrace new methods and changes. It helps you re-program your subconscious so that the subconscious becomes a messenger that receives instructions from the conscious mind.

How to Practice the Pattern Interrupt Technique

To practice this NLP technique:

1. Decide on a particular behavior you wish to change. This has to be something you do automatically without thinking about it. For instance, eating junk food whenever you are watching TV could be an example of something you want to change. Write down in detail in your journal exactly what you would like to change.

2. Start observing how the pattern runs. At what point do you start to experience the urge to eat something? At what point do you decide to get up and walk to the fridge? How do you make a choice of what to eat from the different available choices? Record your decision making process in detail in your journal.

3. Create a pattern interrupt completely alien to the behavior you wish to change. For instance, when you experience the urge to eat something, fold some clothes or instead, drink some water. You need to create a pattern interrupt entirely different from the usual pattern. This pattern interrupt has to jolt you just like the tree that fell in front of your car. Again, write down in detail the new behavior you are going to implement.

4. Every time you feel the urge to engage in the pattern you wish to change, use your pattern interrupt to do something else.

Continue to impose this pattern interrupt and before you know it, you will eliminate the habit you want to change and the new habit will replace the old one (as such, the new habit has to be a positive one). You can use pattern interrupt to get rid of addictions and any negative behavior you wish to eliminate from your person. Reflect on the effectiveness of this technique and how it is influencing your behavior.

3rd NLP Technique: The Swish Technique

The Swish NLP technique helps you alter how your memories affect you. It helps you disconnect from powerful negative thoughts that provoke negative feelings that may negatively affect you and your life.

You can use the swish NLP technique to manage your thoughts and feelings especially thoughts and feelings related to the things happening around you. This NLP technique helps you disconnect from past thoughts such as things that irritated you or made you feel embarrassed in the past, present feelings caused by self-undermining thoughts, and anxieties about forthcoming or future situations.

For instance, if due to illness or stress, you take a leave from work and you find yourself worrying about getting back to work, you have an unwanted negative feeling that in this case, is worry. Each time you remember you have to walk into your office when you resume work next week, your stomach churns and your heart starts racing. This means that walking into that office is the trigger.

You have checked this feeling to see if there are any rational reasons for your fear, but there are none because you have checked with your employers and everything is good. Now, you do not want to be worried and afraid whenever you think of walking into your office next week. You want to be confident and enthusiastic about it.

You can use the Swish technique to replace these feelings and change them into positive ones.

How to Use the Swish NLP Technique

To use the swish NLP technique:

1. Identify the feeling you want eliminate.

2. Identify the thoughts or images that provoke the negative feeling.

3. Check if your fears are founded and rational. If they are simply irrational, move on to the next step.

4. Close your eyes.

5. Create a replacement image in your head. This means you should identify how you want to start feeling. It means you should begin to see yourself acting the way you want.

Now, what you want to do is to point your thoughts towards a fresher and more positive direction. The idea is to re-program your brain by changing the trigger so you can know when you should start thinking new thoughts.

6. Think of the trigger image (the negative one) then start inserting the replacement image in between the trigger image. In between worrying, start

imagining yourself feeling more confident. Before you begin, write down your replacement image in as much detail as you can, to help you solidify your visualization.

7. Allow the replacement image to become bigger and more vivid so that the trigger image begins a gradual disappearance.

8. Break the state and open your eyes.

9. Start from step 1 and this time, try to insert the replacement faster.

10. Repeat the process about 5-7 times.

11. Test it to see what happens when you try to recall the negative trigger image, you will discover that it becomes more difficult to bring back the negative feeling.

If, however, the negative trigger continues to manifest, the trigger may be more powerful than the Swish technique. In that case, try a stronger technique like the anchoring technique. Reflect on the results of the Swish technique in your journal.

4th NLP Technique: The NLP Framing Technique

The NLP Framing technique draws upon the idea that how you perceive everything depends on your point of view. Framing involves trying to change the meaning you attach to a thing by trying to change its context or setting.

For instance, a person trying to annoy you can seem funny so that, rather than becoming angry, you can start laughing at what the person is doing. The meaning you attach to events and things happening around you is dependent on how you frame it.

You can use your responses and behaviors to change the meaning. Dressing as a skeleton to a Halloween party and dressing the same way to a burial would cast different perceptions even though it is the same costume and the same person wearing it.

NLP reframing helps you change how you see and perceive things happening around you so you can behave in a different way. You can get people to see things differently by reframing events and communication differently to get a different response. By using this technique, you can keep calm in the face of fear and maintain your cool when you should be angry or losing your temper.

How to Use the NLP Framing Technique

To use this NLP technique:

1. First, identify a behavior you consider negative or troubling; a behavior or feeling you would like to eliminate from your persona.

2. Now try to establish a communication with the part creating the behavior or response. This could be a sensation in your body, a picture of another person, a specific sound, or voice: anything that triggers the negative behavior or feeling. Write down both the behavior and any triggers associated with it.

3. Ask yourself what exactly you want- what would you rather feel instead? How would you rather behave? You have to recognize the difference between the feeling/behavior and your intended one.

4. Tap into your creativity to figure out three alternative ways you would rather feel or behave instead of the current negative one or some alternative ways to get your intended outcome.

5. Evaluate your new choices and determine whether they are acceptable or not.

6. Check for objections with other parts. Sometimes, when you change an ingrained behavior or pattern, it affects other parts or aspects of your life. You have to ensure your new choices and desired change do not have unintended consequences.

The framing technique helps you tap into your inner resources so you can behave in a way than is far different and superior to your normal way of thinking. Write down any reflections and results from using this technique.

5th NLP Technique: Mirroring and Building Rapport

Mirroring involves mimicking or copying the behavior, body disposition, or speech patterns of a person you are communicating with.

Note: mirroring is very different from aping someone. Aping is where you copy everything someone does; that is not mirroring, that is rude.

Mirroring is subtle and barely noticeable by the person whose body language and speech patterns you are trying to mimic: it has to seem unconscious.

To Mirror someone, you can mimic his or her:

* Speech patterns

* Body language

* Vocabulary style or specific choices of words

* Pace, tempo, pitch, tone, and volume

Mirroring helps you create rapport with the person you are engaging in communication. It makes it possible for the person to warm up to you, trust you, and understand you. A successful interaction can only happen when you maintain rapport with the person you engage in communication with.

There are two approaches to mirroring: you can emphasize the similarities between you and the person, or you can emphasize the differences. Emphasizing the similarities eliminates resistance and antagonism.

Mirroring is a natural thing that most of us do. For instance, if you are trying to talk to a little child, you may crouch so you and the child can be at the same height, or you may talk slowly so the child hears you and understand you better. This is an example of how we naturally mirror others.

How to Practice the NLP Mirroring Technique

To practice mirroring:

1. Mirroring Body Postures: This involves adjusting some parts of your body (or all your body) to match the other person's body posture. Ensure that the posture is a natural one; otherwise, the mirroring may seem disrespectful. You can mirror a person's head and shoulder positions or other natural poses.

2. Mirroring Breathing Patterns: Another thing you can try to match is the breathing pattern. You can mimic the depth or rate of someone's breathing; however, if this breathing is irregular, you should not mimic someone's breathing pattern.

3. Mirroring Voices: You can try to match the voices of those you communicate with by matching the volume, pace, pitch, and choice of words. This can be a very tricky thing to do, but if you learn to do it subtly, you will be better for it because it will improve your rapport building skills. You do not have to mimic every aspect of a person's speech, but you can speak slowly if the person speaks slowly, or speak in a high tone if the person does so.

4. Mirroring Beliefs and Values: Another way to mimic someone is to try to understand his or her values and believes, and try to see that person's perspective. This is not real mimicry because you do not have to agree with that person's believes and values; you just have to understand him or her and avoid levying judgment. Doing this helps build rapport and makes people more likely to warm up to you.

5. Mirror Language Patterns: You can also mirror a person's language patterns. Marketers and sales representatives commonly use this approach. It makes the person you are communicating with feel understood. What you have to do is to use the same words the person uses or use similar paraphrasing. This ensures the other party feels listened to and understood.

Essentially, mirroring makes the person you are communicating with feel as if you are on the same page. It makes the person feel heard and understood, which ensures the person feels comfortable and at home when conversing with you.

For the next few days, make a habit of mirroring and matching people when communicating. Write down your results and observations. Did it improve your communications? How so?

Chapter 4: Psychology of Influence, Persuasion And Manipulation

Manipulation literally means using something as a tool to suit your own purposes. The act of manipulating others typically involves using other people as tools. You can't have remorse or shame if you want to be a successful manipulator. You need to view people as pawns that you move around the board game of life. People are very useful; why not use them?

Manipulation has a bad reputation. It's a dark art because it involves making people act against their will or without their knowledge. Nevertheless, this does not mean that manipulation is always used for bad. Sometimes you might use manipulation for positive purposes, such as causing people to make wise decisions. It can benefit the person that you are manipulating as well as yourself. Sometimes manipulation only benefits only you, but it does not harm the other person. You don't have to use manipulation to hurt others, though it is certainly useful in that respect. Manipulation is a valuable skill to possess because it really helps you gain the upper hand and get what you want. It enables you to use people to their full capacity to further your own goals and aspirations.

It is crucial to be sneaky when you manipulate others. People hate being manipulated and made to do things that they do not consent to. But keep in mind that most people have manipulative tendencies and manipulation is far from rare. Therefore, you are not a bad person for using the manipulation tactics included in this chapter. You are simply going after what you want. That makes you powerful and even positive. Just make sure to hide your manipulation attempts and disguise your intentions. Otherwise, people will judge you harshly and get mad at you. You can lose friends left and right if you gain the reputation of a manipulator. We talk more about hiding your manipulative tendencies and actions in Chapter 8 and Chapter 10, but we talk a little about this in this chapter too.

Dark Psychology

So let's delve into this fascinating and useful subject, shall we?

Make Someone Your Pawn

You can't just manipulate people with whom you don't share a rapport. You have to build a rapport and prime your subject before you can successfully manipulate him. This means that you need to form some sort of relationship with the person. Using a combination of psychological tricks, you can make a person weak for you. Your subject will be willing to do anything for you if you break down his mind and soften him to your attempts at manipulation.

Priming is best achieved through emotional manipulation. You want to play with someone's emotions. The first step is to make someone feel great around you. When someone likes you, he will be more open to your persuasive attempts and will want to please you. He will want to spend time around you because you make him feel good. This time enables you to get your hooks into his mind more successfully. So start with meaningful flattery. Observe your subject to see what means a lot to him. Then compliment him on the things that he values and cares about. For instance, if he loves sports and plays softball on the weekends, talk about sports with him and compliment his pitching techniques or his athletic physique. Over time, he will become increasingly attached to you.

Next, start the emotional roller coaster. As you get to know this person better and make him feel more and more attached to you, start to make him doubt his self-esteem. You can do this by finding things that he is guilty about, or making him feel guilty about things that he does. Always play the victim and make him feel like a terrible person. It's possible to pout like a child but it's even better to act like an adult and pretend to get very hurt about small things he does while telling him that you forgive him. You will look better if you pretend to be an adult who always takes the high road. He will become even more infatuated with you and may start to admire you.

Guilt is very powerful. But so is self-doubt. Plant seeds of doubt in his mind so that he feels insecure. Make him start to hate his friends and family by telling him about horrible things they do or say so that he doubts his social support network and his value to other people. Cause him to question his abilities and skills by saying things like, "You know that you're not good at that!" or "That's not one of your strengths." Tell him that you are simply opening his eyes to his inabilities so that you can protect him from the pain of failure or the pain of being around his hurtful loved ones. Then follow each little insult up with compliments. This will make him very confused. He will start to doubt himself and he will believe what you say because he is attached to you. People are quite sensitive to suggestion, so this method works incredibly well. Meanwhile, he still feels like you are a nice person who cares about him. He won't be ready to end all contact with you just because you insult him from time to time.

You also want to provide him with multiple rewards for what he does for you. When he pleases you, show it and lavish him with praise or favors. Also do favors for him and provide him with lots of services or support so that he is more open to doing favors for you. This is the basic principle of reciprocity, where people like to return kindness and favors that others do for them. You can use the things that you do for him as a bargaining tool. Call on him to return a favor sometime, and he will likely be willing to reciprocate. If he is not willing, guilt him by reminding him of a favor you did for him a while back.

The final part of priming is making someone doubt his sanity and perception. Tell him how he is wrong and come up with convincing arguments as to why. Inform him that he is making things up or misremembering things all of the time. Over time, this will chip away at his security and certainty in his own mind. This method is known as gaslighting, and it is one of the best ways that you can prime someone. Don't take gaslighting lightly. You can use it to totally drive someone crazy over time. It's actually a great form of psychological warfare against someone close to you.

Even if you care about someone, you can still prime him without hurting him. Make him dependent on you so that he never leaves your side. You don't have to be romantically linked to someone to accomplish this sort of dependency. Just offer him something that he can't get anywhere else. Make yourself very useful to him and bolster his ego so that he relies on you for his happiness, convenience, or even financial stability. Disable his other forms of support so that you become the only person in his life. You don't necessarily need to use gaslighting, guilt trips, and other such methods to hurt him; being nice is enough to gain a foothold on someone for persuasive methods. As a friend, lover, or even co-worker, you can accomplish this priming at varying levels. You can do it lightly to someone whom you want to manipulate only slightly. Or you can do it very heavily to someone whom you want to use for life.

Get a Good Read on Someone

There is another side to priming that you really need to take into account. This side is reading. To manipulate someone, you must get a good read on someone. Natural manipulators are adept at reading people at a glance. If you are not so good at reading people right off the bat, then you can use time and priming to get a good read on your subject.

Basically, you want to get to know the person very well. Listen to everything he tells you and glean his speech for potential emotional weapons to use against him. Anything he confides in you or accidentally reveals to you can be turned into a weapon at any time. Save these weapons in your back pocket for when you need to use them.

What are the best emotional weapons? Guilt is probably the most powerful one of all. People hate feeling guilty. So find out things that he feels guilty about.

Also find out things that he loves or cherishes. You can give him these things to make him happy and reward him for his work for you. Or you can cripple him by destroying these things. Love and passion give people power and a will to live. Taking these things away can crush a person. Try to become the gatekeeper of the things that he loves so that you can gain ultimate power over him. For example, bar his access to his loved ones and pitch a fit when he talks to people that you don't approve of, but let him talk to the people he loves whenever he does what you want.

Another way to use what someone loves against him is to trivialize things that he cares about. If he says how much he loves a dish, tell him how it is really not that good. Ruin the small things that he loves. Then you can move on to bigger things. Also, trivialize his opinions. All people love and value their own opinions and believe that they are right. If you make him feel stupid for having certain opinions, then you will be able to chip down his self-esteem and make him doubt his rightness. Make him feel small by trivializing him in every way possible. Eventually, he will come around to your way of thinking and will love only the things that you love because you have made him abandon all that he loves. You will make him feel small and stupid so he will look to you for validation and approval in order to repair his damaged ego.

Trust is a great weapon that you can use. Most people desire to be trusted. You can tell him that he is not trustworthy because of various things that he has admitted to. Then make him do what you want for the sake of winning your trust. Let's say you're dating a guy and you want to manipulate him. Tell him that you don't trust him because he admitted to cheating on his ex. Tell him that you worry he will cheat on you. Or claim that you have been cheated on, so now you have trust issues. This way, he will want to win your trust. He will jump through hoops to make you trust him, including cutting off people you don't like in his life. You can make him cut off female friends and friends who encourage him to drink and have a good time without you around by saying that you feel threatened by these people.

You can also use his reputation to manipulate him. He wants to be liked by others, so you can use that as a weapon. Tell him, "If you do that, everyone at work will hate you. You don't want that, right?" Most likely, if he's a normal person, he will agree that he wants people to like him so he will reconsider doing anything that might damage his reputation. Encourage him to do things by saying that it will gain him favor with different key people. One great way to manipulate co-workers is to give them "tips" on how to please the boss and possibly earn raises or promotions.

Insecurities are fantastic weapons. Whatever hurts him will become apparent rather quickly as you get to know him. Some people are so obvious about their insecurities that you will be able to read what they hate about themselves right away. When someone becomes quiet after a certain subject is brought up, you can bet that he feels insecure about that subject. You can also guess what bothers him based on blatant flaws that he has, such as excessive weight or a poor relationship with his wife. But mainly, you will learn his insecurities by listening to him. Listen to what he talks about and notice the things that seem to bother him or that he complains about. These insecurities are things that you can bring up at opportune moments to hurt him. You can also urge him to do things to atone for what he lacks, or to fix a flaw that he perceives in himself. In addition, you can plant new insecurities in his mind by casually mentioning flaws that you notice in him or saying nasty things to him about himself during arguments.

Finally, his level of affection or even love for you is a powerful weapon. This is why friends or lovers will say things like, "If you really love me, you won't do this." This is also why people like to threaten to leave. You can threaten to withdraw your love from him to goad him into action.

Play the Victim

Playing the victim is your number one "get out of jail free" card in life. If you become adept at playing the victim, you can pretty much justify anything that you do and make your subject feel terrible about anything that he does.

First of all, you want to believe that you are the victim. You can accomplish this by rationalizing things. Use your conscious processes to justify your actions. Think of ways that others have wronged you in order to excuse your actions. As long as you believe that you are the victim, then you won't feel guilty about playing the victim card.

You also want to establish your innocence and vulnerability. You want to appear like an innocent victim being harmed by life so that others feel sorry for you. Tell people sob stories about how the world is against you. Make sure that your situations are not self-imposed so that others don't get irritated and think that you just blame others for your own problems. A good example of this is talking about how you were abused as a child so that you can explain why you have difficulties picking good love partners and healthy friends now. This excuses your actions and makes you seem like a victim who cannot control your own mind or help yourself. Strike sympathy in others so that people want to support you.

When your subject does anything that you don't like, play the victim card. Show him how deeply he has hurt you. You won't accomplish this by pouting, giving him the silent treatment, or throwing a wild tantrum. You will enjoy way more success playing the victim card if you appear mature and calm about something. Inform him in a steady voice that he has hurt you. Offer him consequences for his actions that he won't like. Say that you feel the need to protect your heart and your interests from him. Also, make him feel like a monster by continuing to appear like a saint who never does any wrong. You don't want to do something wrong to him that he can use as a weapon against you when you play the victim card.

Let's revisit cheating in a romantic partnership. If you want to prevent him from cheating, you can play the victim card when he talks to or looks at other women. But be very cautious that you never do anything with another person that makes you look bad. If you do cheat, make sure that he never, ever even suspects you of what you did. Never let him access texts or social media posts that he can use against you, or your whole victim plan will fall apart.

You can also very effectively play the victim card by telling other people what he does to you. Act as if you aren't complaining about him. Just casually mention things that he does that are abhorrent. Blow what he did out of proportion to make him seem terrible, but don't make it obvious that you are trying to complain about him. Instead, make it seem like you are the victim of his actions and you don't realize that you have been terribly wronged. Other people will become shocked and even outraged that he would do this to poor little innocent you. They may even become your soldiers, confronting him and making him feel guilty.

Guilt is your best trump card. Use it well. But also use it wisely. Playing the victim card too often will wear out its power.

Dr. Cialdini's Six Principles of Influence

You can use the Six Principles of Influence to influence any person to do what you want. These six principles are the foundation blocks of persuasion and manipulation. Keep them in mind and use them to gain influence over others. You can get what you want by using these principles.

The first principle is the reciprocity that we already discussed. Basically, you want to make people feel as if they owe you. Do favors for people so that you can call on them later when you need something. Appear very warm and generous so that others want to do things for you.

The second principle involves social proof. You basically want to be well-liked. The more popular you are, the more influence you have. Other people will back you up if you are well-liked. And new people that you meet will want to do things for you to gain your favor, since everyone else likes you.

Dark Psychology

Commitment and consistency is the third principle. People tend to stick to things that they know. They like consistency. So you can appeal to someone by asking him to do something that he already does. This works well in sales – if you have a customer who always likes the same types of products, you should target him with similar products. Brand loyalty is built upon this principle.

Authority grants you a lot of influence. If you appear like an authority figure, others will do what you say. The infamous Milton Prison Experiment is a classic example of how people are willing to obey authority figures to great lengths. Appear like you know what you are doing and be bossy. People will believe that you have more power than you really do if you act like it.

Scarcity is where you can essentially scare someone into action. Let your subject know that something is in limited supply. He will jump into action to get it before it runs out. This is the principle at play when TV commercials command you to act fast before supplies run out.

Liking is the final principle. This is where you want to make people like you. Being a kind, sincere person (at least on the outside) can make others want to do things for you. Also, appearing warm will make people like you. Approach someone with a proposal or favor in a warm room or offer him a warm drink to give the impression that you are warm. Use light touch, such as an arm brushing during conversation, and lots of eye contact to establish a bond. In Eastern cultures and some Native American cultures, eye contact and touch is not encouraged, so instead you want to appear deferent and deeply respectful at all times, keep your hands to yourself, and avoid eye contact.

Denial

Denial is extremely powerful. People don't want to believe things that hurt them. So they put up fronts and convince themselves that reality is just peachy. You can use denial to your favor when you are manipulating someone.

One way to use denial is to justify your own behavior to yourself. You won't be a great manipulator if you feel bad about what you're doing. You need to justify what you are doing to yourself. Denying the level of depravity that you have sunk to is a great way to do this.

Another thing that you can use denial for is manipulating your subject. Use his own sense of denial against him. Tell him that he is in denial about things to convince him that he is in the wrong. Make him think that you know him better than he knows himself. That will make him rely on you yet more for affirmation and validation of himself. It will also make him start to doubt himself and wonder what it is that he is in denial about.

Finally, denial is great for defending yourself. Vehemently deny any and all wrongdoing. Should someone accuse you of being less than upfront and trying to manipulate others, deny it. Never admit to any wrongdoing. You want to appear like you have done nothing wrong. This will make your subject believe it. If you stand steadfastly beside your innocence, you will appear more innocent. Eventually, your subject may cave and rethink his accusations. He may even stop suspecting you of any wrongdoing. Use this opportunity to convince him that he is just seeing things or being too sensitive or thinking of a past friend, lover, or family member who was manipulative to him. Tell him that he is projecting stuff onto you and that it isn't fair to you. Again, you want to whip out that victim card and even convince yourself that you are a victim. This makes the denial even more complete.

Chapter 5: Brainwash and Hypnotism

Hypnotism Is Real

Of all the aspects of dark psychology presented in this book, hypnotism is the one most likely to raise eyebrows. When most people hear the word "hypnotism" they think of a guy with a moustache and a top hat waving a pocket watch while insisting someone is "getting very sleepy." Believing in this stereotype is actually dangerous. This is because real hypnotists are out there and are equipped with subtle but powerful techniques. These people are able to draw upon the darkest elements of psychology to influence people in an incredibly powerful way.

So if hypnotism isn't the old stereotypical image of a stage hypnotist, what exactly is hypnosis? Simply put, it is the ability to make suggestions to someone that filter through deep layers of their consciousness. This ability to make deep, impactful suggestions to someone while they are in a vulnerable and suggestible state grants hypnotic dark manipulators a high level of power over their victims. Unlike almost every other technique in this book, hypnotism is not something that people encounter in a milder, more innocent form in their day-to-day lives.

Hypnotism can take the form of both verbal and nonverbal suggestive practices. Often, the forms of suggestion are very subtle and therefore difficult to detect. By its very nature, hypnosis works on the deepest levels of a person's mind. Someone who is skilled in generating a hypnotic state and response in someone will be able to bypass their defenses and influence them without raising any alarms or giving a person a chance to raise their guard.

Hypnotic Tactics

Now that you understand the difference between the stereotype of what hypnosis is, and what it actually is, it is time to explore the main hypnotic tactics. There are many variations on these types of tactics but they offer an insight into the main things to be wary of. Examples of how each tactic can be used will be provided wherever possible to give a clear insight into how hypnotists operate in our midst, undetected, every day.

Suggestion Can Be Silent

If hypnotism, in a darkly psychological sense of the word, can be understood as "deep suggestion," then it is important to understand what exactly is meant by suggestion in this instance. Most people might imagine a suggestion is a clearly stated statement like "I suggest you do this." This is far from the truth. The dark psychology view of suggestion is very far apart from the usual understanding of the word. The first important concept to grasp is the fact that hypnotic suggestion can be either verbal or nonverbal.

Picture the human brain as an iceberg. The part of the iceberg that is above the surface of the water represents the known and understood aspects of cognitive function such as thought. The larger, deeper part of the ice submerged below the water represents parts of the brain that are consciously inaccessible and little understood. If you doubt the power of this hidden portion of the brain you need only think of dreaming and the immense power of the mind to generate series of images, pictures, and sounds while a person is asleep. Dark hypnotists target their efforts toward this hidden, subconscious part of the mind.

There are, broadly speaking, two types of suggestion used by hypnotists—silent and verbal. Both types of hypnotic technique come in a variety of different forms. The exact type of hypnotism a manipulative person chooses to use at any given time depends on a range of factors. Some manipulators will carry out whichever form of hypnotism they feel will be most impactful on their victim's particular psyche. Others carry out whichever technique they happen to wish to use for their own amusement at the time. This depends largely on whether the hypnotist is seeking to exert influence in the most powerful way possible or is merely trying to control someone for their own fun and games.

Verbal suggestion is very difficult to detect. Sometimes, dark hypnotists are able to implant suggestions into their victim's mind using words that sound similar to other, more innocent words.

To take a deeply dark example, if a hypnotist was trying to instill suicidal feelings in their target, they may mask the true command of "You want to die" as something similar sounding such as "You want to dine." The hypnotist would speak the words "you want to die" clearly, but in a context that would mask the true content. For example, the hypnotist could talk about an upcoming trip and state "You have to check out the local restaurants, you want to die, somewhere that is popular but picturesque." The victim's mind would absorb the suggestion of death without consciously understanding why!

The above example of masked verbal suggestions is akin to a poison being hidden in someone's food. The victim consumes the hidden content, thinking that they are enjoying something helpful and innocuous when in actual fact they are absorbing something deadly. The especially devastating part of this technique is the fact the victim will never notice it. Even if someone thought they had picked up on the true words the hypnotist had spoken, imagine how crazy they would sound calling them out! People will generally take whichever option is psychologically easier for them and will therefore accept the masked command without question.

A hypnotist's tone of voice and choice of words is another method of verbal suggestion. Some hypnotists will carefully learn the pace and style of delivery a particular victim uses when they are expressing something serious.

For example, if, when someone wishes to say something meaningful, their voice lowers in pitch and slows in pace, the hypnotist would memorize this detail and retain it for future use. The hypnotist would then make suggestions to the victim in that exact, mirrored tone of voice. Because of the carefully modulated tone, the words delivered in that vocal variation would deeply penetrate a victim's defenses. Because the hypnotist would only deliver the suggestive content in that tone of voice, and then switch back to their usual way of speaking, the victim would be unaware even of what had taken place.

Another form of personalized, verbal suggestion employed by a hypnotic user of dark psychology is to pick up on words that have a special, intense significance for the victim who uses them. For example, when someone is very emotional they will often use a particular term to convey this feeling. If the hypnotic manipulator is able to pick up on these personal words then they are able to deploy them for their own benefit. Just as people have a specific tone of voice, they have a list of personal words of meaning, without often knowing it. The manipulator will understand their victim better than the victim understands herself. Knowing these words and tones, the manipulator can reverse engineer the victim's own brain to use against them.

Suggestion can also take nonverbal forms as well. This can be through the hypnotic manipulator's body language or even cues they place in their environment. If you think such seemingly trivial things could not exert a hypnotic influence then think again! Even political leaders have made use of such tactics in ways such as changing their hairstyle to convey a different intention during speeches. As discomforting as it is to believe, the human mind is deeply susceptible to even the smallest hints and cues.

So what are some of the main ways a hypnotic manipulator can use nonverbal suggestion against their victim? The technique centers around the idea of association. A skilled hypnotist is able to consistently link a strong emotion to some kind of external stimulus such as a particular eye movement they use. For example, if a hypnotist wanted to be able to trigger a feeling of panic in a victim, they may choose to make a particular motion with their eyes whenever the victim was thinking about, or experiencing, panic. The victim's subconscious would then learn to link the eye movement to the feeling. Over time, the hypnotist would be able to trigger the emotional response simply by making the eye movement, even without the need for any other stimulus.

Environmental stimulus is another form of nonverbal suggestion that forms a part of the hypnotist's toolkit. Think of environmental stimulus as like being summoned to the principal's office as a child. The location itself was enough to send you into a feeling of deep panic because you had learned to associate the location with panic and problems. Hypnotists are able to use this same concept to devastating effect in adult life.

For example, they will often be sure to have a certain type of conversation with a victim in one location only. Picture a hypnotist and their victim in a romantic relationship. Every time the hypnotist wishes to get some kind of agreement or consent from his victim, he may be sure to ask her only when they are at a certain coffee shop. Over a period of time, the victim's mind begins to associate the physical environment of the coffee shop with the granting of permission. The hypnotist can then use this physical environment as external psychological leverage whenever he needs to exert influence and control.

Vulnerable Victims

Hypnotism is not equally effective on everybody it is tried on. Some people are more likely to be influenced by a hypnotist than others. Although the exact level of susceptibility is complex and hard to simplify in a single sentence, it boils down to the idea of vulnerability. Vulnerable people are more likely to be agreeable to hypnotic suggestion than people who are less vulnerable. The types of vulnerability sought out by hypnotists in their victims will now be explored along with a guide to how hypnotists exacerbate and magnify the vulnerable paradigm.

The people most vulnerable to hypnotism are those who have recently experienced a significant life-changing event that has reduced their stability and certainty. For example, if a person has just come out of a serious romantic relationship, has suffered bereavement or lost their job, they are particularly vulnerable to suggestion. This is because the human brain craves certainty and understanding above all else. If a hypnotist spots someone who is in a vulnerable place they can offer them certainty and change their vulnerability in general to vulnerability around the hypnotist specifically.

There are roughly two facets of vulnerability in a hypnotist's victim—preexisting vulnerability and exacerbated vulnerability. The most diabolical hypnotists are able to combine both aspects to lethal effect. Not only will the best hypnotic manipulators be able to find someone who is suitably vulnerable, they will find someone who is specifically vulnerable to the hypnotic psychological scheme they have planned.

For example, if a hypnotist is looking to use their powers to gain financially, they might seek out a victim such as a rich, recently bereaved widow. They will then, subtly and over time, associate their own self with feelings of security and comfort while increasing the widow's general feelings of loss and vulnerability. Eventually, the hypnotist is the victim's only refuge from a hell of their own making.

As well as seeking out vulnerability in general, hypnotists are known to seek out situational vulnerability as well. This is when someone is in a situational circumstance that makes them more suggestible than their overall "baseline" of suggestibility. There are tactical tricks a hypnotist can use to ascertain this situational vulnerability. One such tactic is trying to induce "mirroring" behavior in their target. When people feel a subconscious level of connection and rapport with someone they will start to "mirror" the person without knowing they are doing it. To check this, a hypnotist might make some small change to their body language, such as a hand motion. If the victim subconsciously mimics this gesture, then it is a sign the victim is situationally vulnerable.

Now that both general and situational vulnerability have been explored, it is important to understand how the most skilled hypnotists use the two types of vulnerability together for an especially strong impact. If someone is vulnerable in general, due to their life situation, and vulnerable in particular, due to the situation the hypnotist has managed to set up, then that person is in the most influenceable state imaginable. Once such a state has been induced the hypnotist is likely to move on to the most powerful and advanced techniques they possess, such as NLP.

NLP

NLP, or neurolinguistic programming, is a technique that is powerful even in the hands of the most well-intentioned people. Leaders within the world of business and philanthropy are some of the most common advocates of the techniques and principles offered by NLP. Placing such techniques in the hands of people willing to use dark psychology to exploit others is like giving a nuclear weapon to a psychopath. They possess both the power and the will to create serious psychological havoc among their victims. Understanding the main techniques used by practitioners of dark psychology offers insight into the way they can be deployed to devastating impact.

Anchoring

Anchoring is an NLP technique that involves linking an emotional state to some form of external stimulus. If you are familiar with the idea of Pavlovian conditioning, then you will understand this tactic. Hypnotists are able to induce a powerful emotion in a victim and then link it to a stimulus such as a physical gesture or tone of voice. The hypnotist is then able to induce this emotional state at will by performing the linked stimulus.

The most nefarious hypnotists will use the principle of anchoring in a very subtle and underhand way. They will work for a prolonged period of time to induce a variety of different anchors in the psyche of their victim without the victim's conscious awareness of what is taking place. This provides the manipulator with a set of hypnotic puppet strings that they can pull as and when they desire. Often, hypnotists will use an "anchor stack" to induce different intense feelings in quick succession. For example, they will induce the feeling of love, followed by terror, followed by love once more, all in quick succession. This series of emotions overloads the victim's emotional circuitry and leaves them as mere clay in the hands of their controller.

Reframing

Reframing is the art of controlling the way ambiguous information is perceived. There is an old saying that "nothing is good or bad unless we believe it to be." Reframing is the ultimate technique related to this idea. Hypnotists can use reframing to effectively control the way their victim thinks and feels. Think of a skilled reframer as an editor. They are able to selectively choose the victim's focus and the feelings the focus triggers. This is effectively hypnotic mind control.

So how does darkly psychological reframing work in practice? Let's take a situation where a hypnotic manipulator has influenced a victim to no longer spend time around, or communicating with, a particular person. The victim may state feelings of sadness or loss related to this interpersonal change. The hypnotist would be able to reframe these feelings into ones which suited the hypnotist's own purposes. This is best illustrated through an example dialogue.

Dark Psychology

Victim - "It sucks I haven't spoken to Rachel as much, I miss her."

Hypnotist - "I know you might hate how things are with Rachel, but I know you're smart enough to love the freedom you have now."

Notice how the concept of hate is linked to Rachel and love is linked to the "freedom" of being without her? The hypnotist also plays on the victim's ego by linking the idea of their intelligence to going along with the way the hypnotist wants them to perceive the "frame," or perception, of the facts. Think about what you have already learned about the vulnerability of victims and you will understand how this reframing can be used to devastating impact.

Future Pacing

Future pacing is the closest thing possible to psychologically manipulative time travel. Future pacing allows a skilled manipulator to lead their victim on a mental journey into the future and influence behaviors and responses that will occur in the actual, chronological future that exists independent of the victim's reality.

At its most fundamental, future pacing involves the mental leading of a victim through a future scenario. For example, if the hypnotist wants their victim to feel generous and relaxed whenever they receive money, the hypnotist would ask their victim to envision a situation, such as receiving their next paycheck. To make this future imagining possible the hypnotist would ensure the victim imagined all of their five senses in action—what they would see, feel, touch etc. at the time. This helps the brain to perceive the future scenario as "real" due to its sensory depth.

Once the hypnotist cognitively transports their victim into the future, they begin to suggest certain happenings and monitor the responses. For example, the hypnotist may say something like "Imagine being very generous with this paycheck and providing it to those who really need it, because you are a kind person and doing the right thing is deep in your nature." If the victim's physical response to this future scenario showed signs of compliance and acceptance then the hypnotic manipulator would have the confidence that their victim would actually behave in this way when the scenario occurs in the future.

Due to the intensity and power of the hypnotic techniques mentioned in this chapter, the best manipulators only use them in moderation. For example, a darkly psychological hypnotist would be sure to keep their interaction with a victim 95% normal. This will increase the victim's comfort and trust to such high levels that the 5% time spent on hypnotic influence would not only slip past a victim's defenses unnoticed but would work to great effect once embedded in the victim's mind.

Brainwashing

Are You Brainwashed About Brainwashing?

If you ask someone if they know what brainwashing is, they will probably reply that they do. Brainwashing is a concept that many people have heard of, while mistaking their vague familiarity for accurate understanding. Before looking at how, where, and why brainwashing occurs, it is essential to understand exactly what brainwashing is and isn't. Of all the dark psychology techniques contained in this book, brainwashing has the most serious and widest impact. If the other dark psychology techniques are sniper bullets, aimed at one particular person, brainwashing is a nuclear bomb capable of devastating an entire city.

The term brainwashing refers to the slow process of replacing a person's ideas about identity and belief with new ideas that are intended to suit the purpose of the person doing the brainwashing. Brainwashing can occur in both wider and narrower contexts. For example, a brainwasher is able to control one person in particular, or use the same techniques and principles to control the minds of a wider group at once. Brainwashing is the process that turns atheists into suicide bombers and prisoners of war into communists. It has been tried, tested, and proven over the years to be effective in almost any scenario.

So what are the most common misunderstandings related to brainwashing? Many people picture the process as some kind of quick and forced occurrence. Picture either Alex in "A Clockwork Orange" or Neo in "The

Matrix" having concepts forced into their cranium, involuntarily, in a short space of time. This is Hollywood brainwashing and is far from what actually occurs in real life.

The process of real-world brainwashing will be explored in detail later in this chapter, but at its simplest, brainwashing is a process involving the slow, gradual, and seemingly voluntary changing of a person's "map of reality" from the one they have freely put together to one that is forced upon them by the brainwasher. The evil irony of the technique is the brainwasher will ensure the victim feels in control at all times.

Brainwashing Contexts

So what are some of the main situations that are fertile breeding grounds for brainwashers? Before the process of brainwashing itself is explored fully, let's take a look at the situations in which people are often brainwashed and the motivations behind this.

A lot of people would agree with the idea that "cults brainwash people" but few would be able to explain exactly what a cult is and how they brainwash their recruits. Let's demystify the process. A cult is a fringe group, often built around a charismatic leader who is able to exert high levels of influence over their followers. The cult will usually provide a "complete understanding of reality" to those who follow it. Why exactly is this cult context one in which brainwashing flourishes?

The primary attraction of cults is they present reality as something very simple and within reach of the average person, provided the person is willing to take on board the cult's teachings. We live in a complex modern world where life can seem confusing and overwhelming. Cults cut through this confusion and tell people "don't worry, we have the answer." The way in which this "answer" is presented is intended to play on the human need for belonging and acceptance. Brainwashing can flourish in this context as a result of the idea of the "new normal."

What exactly is "the new normal"? It is a way in which cults are able to influence those they brainwash into accepting their teachings by making them seem prevalent, accepted and positive. For example, the idea of worshipping a man who claims to be God would be incredibly strange in everyday life. Within the closed environment of a cult, however, this behavior becomes "normal" to the extent that not doing it would seem strange to people within the cult! This process of persistent, social reinforcement is one of the most powerful ways in which the ideological brainwashing of cults is able to occur.

Think of cults as drug dealers. Perhaps the newcomer to the cult had been seeking something in their life and came across the cult, just as newcomers to the world of drugs often, misguidedly, seek out their first high of their own volition. The cult doesn't need to "push" the drug of their ideology onto the victim as the victim was already seeking the fulfillment of a void in their life. It is this initial "search" and "readiness" on the part of the people who are later brainwashed that makes them so susceptible to the brainwashing process itself.

Ideologies are another context, similar to cults, in which brainwashing is commonplace. The difference between a cult and an ideology is the focus of the ideology is on the idea itself rather than the person delivering the message and those who follow them. Whereas cults brainwash people into placing faith and trust in the cult leader and their followers, ideological brainwashing involves leading people to place absolute trust in an idea.

Ideological brainwashing is incredibly dangerous due to the fact it goes above and beyond any one individual. Think of extremist religious terrorism, for example. It is possible for a high profile figure within the ideology, such as Osama Bin Laden, to be killed. Does this kill support for the idea itself? No! The dead figures are praised as martyrs who gave their life to the ideology, thus increasing its attractiveness and allure to potential newcomers.

Almost any ideology is likely to have an extremist, fringe outskirt in which brainwashing takes place. Even something seemingly innocent like a pop band can have this impact. Young fans, at a psychologically impressionable age, link their sense of identity, happiness, and belonging to a pop group. They will gladly defend this group to extents that are unusually intense. Some pop groups have fans that even self-harm, using razor blades, if a member quits the group! If you carefully consider this phenomenon of the power of brainwashing even in accidental, innocent contexts, then consider how devastating the process can be in intended contexts like cults and terrorist groups.

Now that you have a clear understanding of the way brainwashing can occur in broader social contexts, such as cults and ideologies, it is important to understand that a personal, one-on-one context is also a ripe situation for elements of brainwashing to occur in. There are similarities and differences between "group" and "individual" brainwashing and understanding these nuances can help to identify when either type is occurring.

Personal brainwashing is similar to group brainwashing as it involves the slow and steady replacement of existing beliefs with new beliefs that serve the objectives of the brainwasher. Instead of relying on group dynamics to reinforce "the new normal," a one on one brainwashing situation will instead rely on a deep, personal connection between the brainwasher and the victim. This can be even more powerful than group brainwashing as the content can be modified and altered to the particular psychological constitution of the victim.

The Process Of Brainwashing

Now that you understand the reality of what brainwashing is, and where it occurs, let's take a look at the specific process itself. Distinctions will be drawn between the way in which the process applies to both group and individual situations.

The starting point of any episode of brainwashing is the mental state and social circumstance of the victim. This is the foundation upon which the rest of the process is entirely reliant. Brainwashing is not something that can be carried out on absolutely anyone. It requires the identification of a person who is seeking something or trying to fill a void in their life.

So what kind of people are ideal victims for brainwashers? People who have had their existing reality shaken up by a recent event are prime targets for brainwashers. For example, many of the Western men who have travelled to become terrorists in Syria, and detonate suicide bombs, have done so after the death of a close friend or relative. When their existing world loses its meaning and certainty, brainwashers can step in and provide that certainty in the form of a murderous ideology.

Once a brainwashing victim has been identified, either in person or via the Internet, the actual process of brainwashing begins. Contrary to the popular image of a brainwasher as a wide-eyed psychopath who will incessantly and angrily indoctrinate their victim, real-world brainwashers are anything but this. They will come across as calm, friendly, rational people who have their lives together in a way the victim does not. Imagine being homeless and being befriended by a celebrity. This is how the process of meeting their brainwasher for the first time feels for a victim.

The brainwasher will often work initially on creating a level of trust and rapport between themselves and their victim. This usually involves creating both deep and superficial similarities. For example, superficial similarities may involve surface level preferences like an enjoyment of the same sport or even food! Deeper level rapport may involve some "deep" shared experience in the past of both the brainwasher and the victim. Brainwashers will convincingly fake these if needed. If the victim shares the fact that they have lost a relative in the past, guess what? The brainwasher suddenly has a similar story to tell.

The false emotional warmth and connection explained above is not the only aspect of brainwashing that occurs initially. The brainwasher will often provide gifts and other favors to their victim. For example, the brainwasher may treat them to meals or send them gadgets or other useful items. This creates a sense of gratitude and indebtedness from the victim to their brainwasher and softens up any resistance the victim may initially experience.

One of the most powerful examples of the above initial kindness can be taken from Prisoner of War camps. When American troops have been captured in the past, their captors often offer them American cigarettes and speak to them in a respectful way. This reverses the expectations of the victim and opens the victim's mind to the further brainwashing process that is to follow.

A utopian presentation is the next step in the brainwashing process, following the initial victim identification and rapport building stages. This involves the brainwasher slowly and increasingly offering a solution to all of the problems that the victim has opened up about. This is always done in a casual, offhand way at first to avoid any negative experiences of pressure the victim may experience otherwise. This utopian solution is always whatever cult, ideology or personality the brainwasher is trying to convert their victim to—terrorism, communism or just a charismatic brainwasher's own need for validation and praise.

When performed correctly, the initial stages of this process will leave a victim craving more and more information and understanding of the solution that is being hinted at. The brainwasher may even withhold this information initially, as if it is something that the victim must work at being worthy of attaining. This will lead to a strong motivation on behalf of the victim to seek out and accept the information they are eventually provided with. Thanks to the preceding steps, the poisonous ideas that are being implanted into the victim will seem as natural and refreshing as cold water on a hot day.

Once the victim is being spoon fed snippets of their new belief system, and responding well to them, the brainwasher will be very careful to reveal the right things at the right time. This is a concept that is sometimes known as "milk before meat" or "gradual revelation." It basically involves the presentation of easy to accept ideas before anything controversial is revealed. For example, in the case of religious terrorism, recruiters may initially focus on convincing their victim that God loves them. This is usually quite acceptable. More objectionable ideas, such as God wants you to blow yourself up, are saved until far further down the line. At this point, the brainwashing has reached the point of no return.

You may be questioning way a victim continues to engage with their brainwasher once the objectionable ideas begin to become apparent. The reason is threefold. First, the already vulnerable victim now feels a strong sense of liking and approval of their brainwasher.

Second, the victim has invested time and sometimes money into the process thus far. This is known as the "sunk cost fallacy." The victim is loath to "throw away all their hard work" by walking away from the process.

Finally, the brainwasher is likely to have amassed a lot of secretive and sensitive information on their victim. This "dirt" can then be held over the victim's head, either discreetly or overtly.

Both the ideas of a vulnerable victim and the "sunk cost fallacy" make logical sense. The idea of blackmail and control may be harder to understand at first. Why would a victim respond well to such threats? Well, they are rarely presented in a threatening way. For example, if the victim has divulged a lot of sensitive information to a brainwasher, and then begins to give signs of walking away, the brainwasher may appear concerned and insist that "if I can't help you anymore with your problems, I need to make sure someone else can. Perhaps your family or boss need to know what's been going on with you, so they can look out for you when I'm not there."

Because of the deep sense of rapport and warmth the brainwasher has manipulated their victim into feeling, the above form of blackmail and control is often actually perceived as kind, compassionate behavior. It is often enough to make the victim see "sense" and agree to remain on the brainwashing path they have embarked upon. Brainwashers are adept at making the pain and struggle of walking away seem epic, so staying becomes the preferable, easy option by default.

The end product of this process is the victim believing everything they have been indoctrinated to view as the truth. The power of the process is that the victim will feel they have chosen these views as their own and have sought them out through their own volition. This leaves a previously normal individual as an indoctrinated psychological slave to something they have no idea even exists.

The Impact Of Brainwashing

The above analysis of the brainwashing process shows the severity and depth of the technique. It is inevitable that a process as powerful as this has lasting consequences. Some of the main impacts of brainwashing after the process has been completed will now be explored.

Loss of identity is one of the most serious side effects of brainwashing. A feature of many cults and ideologies is that people who complete their initiation process are given a new name. This allows the person's psyche to totally detach from their old identity. They can believe things and do things they would never have done before as the person they used to be no longer exists. When carried out carefully the brainwashing process leaves a victim feeling as if their old identity was no more real or permanent than a nightmare from which they have awoken.

So is brainwashing simply a process of ideas? Not at all. If brainwashing resulted in only the change of opinions then it would be far less of a problem than it actually is. The main danger of brainwashing is it not only changes the ways that people think and feel but also the way they behave. People go from functional members of the society with acceptable, positive jobs and interests to brainwashed zombies willing to carry out rape, murder, and suicide. This sounds sensational and dramatic, but it's true. Read on for the proof.

If you have any doubts about what brainwashing can drive a person to, consider the following examples. Members of some religious cults will gladly cut off all contact from their family, leave their careers behind, surrender all their wealth and possessions, and place their autonomy entirely in the hands of the organization that has brainwashed them. This is not all. The victim will see their new lifestyle as a blessing they are fortunate to have, rather than something unpleasant they have been forced into.

Another example of the toxic outcome of brainwashing is the repeated tale of young people becoming brainwashed by religious extremists to travel to a foreign land and drive a car packed full of explosives into a group of people they have never met and who have never hurt them. Such young victims are often educated people with a track record of success in life and a family history free of turmoil or abuse. These tragic losses of life are testament to the overwhelming, all-conquering power of the brainwashing process.

PTSD (post traumatic stress disorder) is another hallmark of those who manage to escape, or are rescued from, a situation of intense brainwashing.

Dark Psychology

Brainwashing victims often show the same physical and psychological signs as war veterans who have witnessed their friends being blown apart next to them during combat. The severity of this traumatic aftermath shows that a brainwashing situation can harm a person as much as a world war.

Perhaps the most shocking examples of the long-term impact of brainwashing are the numerous instances of people who have been rescued or escaped from a brainwashing situation, only to later return of their own free will. Even once they are outside of the controlling, brainwashing environment, the legacy of the process runs so deep through a person's mind, they seek to return to it. This is a form of Stockholm syndrome. The escapees will actually praise their brainwashers far into the future and defend, support, and justify the ideological stances they were indoctrinated with while captive.

Conclusion

Time to take a deep breath and assimilate all the information presented to you, in this book.

If you are experiencing a stressful time, it can be useful to learn relaxation techniques. They will help you manage your mental wellbeing. Many of these can be done in the privacy of your own home, or even in a work situation.

Your mental wellbeing is as important as your physical health. It plays an important role in your happiness. You owe it to yourself to break out of any unhealthy stronghold that others might place on you, such as a manipulative character. No one could be happy living or working alongside another person who belittles them. Most particularly if that person coerces them into doing something they don't want to do. That is exactly what living with a controlling person is like, at work or home. You will feel trapped as they slowly destroy your self-esteem. If your partner or work colleague is never open to compromise, then they may well be manipulative and controlling. A healthy relationship, be it personal or work related, should be one whereby everyone feels comfortable.

Most of us grow up to be taught the social rules of good manners and acceptable behavior. Unfortunately, some either ignore this learning process or have no one to teach and guide them. We need positive role models in our informative years. Those who may have suffered abuse either physically or mentally as children, will be scarred in some form or another. Many will still manage a normal life, but it's unlikely that anyone can come out of a bad childhood unscathed.

Many of us struggle on in our daily lives. We perform routine tasks to make our lives pleasant and our loved ones happy. There comes a time when we do not always have the energy or inclination to help other people. Most of us will do a kindness along the way. Always though, our priorities are for our own loved ones. There is a certain necessity to be strong if you wish to make something of your life. Otherwise, depression can set in and you may drown in the many temptations around you. Excessive eating, or even worse the temptations of alcohol and drugs could seem an easy way out.

It does take courage to stand up to a controlling manipulative character, but you must be brave and see it through. Push them away from your life and keep them at arm's length. Don't be taken in by their false promises. If someone encompasses you so tightly that you feel you cannot breathe, then you must escape. A healthy relationship should not feel like that.

This book should enlighten you on how to cope with some of the problems you may face in life. It is meant only as a guide on how to deal with controlling manipulative relationships. It cannot give you your freedom. Only courage can do that. Build up your self-confidence. Take care of your health. For the sake of living a happy life, learn how to handle such controlling characters that may pass you by.